modern PLUS SIGN QUILTS

16 Dynamic Projects

A Variety of Techniques

Cheryl Brickey and Paige Alexander

stashBOOKS.

an imprint of C&T Publishing

Text copyright © 2018 by Cheryl Brickey and Paige Alexander

Photography and artwork copyright © 2018 by C&T Publishing, Inc.

Publisher: Amy Marson

Creative Director: Gailen Runge

Editors: Lynn Koolish and Kathryn Patterson

Technical Editor: Nan Powell

Cover/Book Designer: April Mostek

Production Coordinator: Tim Manibusan

Production Editor: Jennifer Warren

Illustrator: Linda Johnson

Photo Assistant: Mai Yong Vang

Style photography by Lucy Glover and instructional photography by
Diane Pedersen of C&T Publishing, Inc., unless otherwise noted

Published by Stash Books, an imprint of C&T Publishing, Inc., P.O. Box 1456,
Lafayette, CA 94549

Library of Congress Cataloging-in-Publication Data

Names: Brickey, Cheryl, 1978- author. | Alexander, Paige, 1962- author.

Title: Modern plus sign quilts : 16 dynamic projects, a variety of techniques /
Cheryl Brickey and Paige Alexander.

Description: Lafayette, CA : C&T Publishing, Inc., 2018.

Identifiers: LCCN 2017030792 | ISBN 9781617455698 (soft cover)

Subjects: LCSH: Patchwork--Patterns. | Quilting--Patterns. | Crosses--Miscellanea.

Classification: LCC TT835 .B6996 2018 | DDC 746.46/041--dc23

LC record available at https://lccn.loc.gov/2017030792

Printed in China

10 9 8 7 6 5 4 3 2 1

APRIL 2018

acknowledgments

From Cheryl

I would like to thank my wonderful husband, Mike, and my children, Christopher and Sarah, for all their support (and for tolerating quilts in various stages of completion all over the house). Thanks also to my official quilt testers, Abby the cat and Katie the dog.

Many thanks to my parents, Mike and Carole, who gave me my first sewing machine and have always supported me in pursuing my interests and dreams. To all my quilting friends, both local and online, thank you so much for all your inspiration, friendship, and encouragement.

I would also like to thank Paige for joining me on this adventure; there is no one else with whom I would rather have coauthored a book.

From Paige

I owe my love of sewing to my grandmama Sadie, who had the patience to teach me to sew at a young age. I had the best-dressed Barbie in town.

I would like to thank my supportive husband, Jason, who always gave his opinion when asked, knowing all the while it might not be used. And thanks to my parents—especially my mom, Linda Taylor, who prayed for me every stitch along the way. I would also like to thank my friend and fellow quilter, Linda Cassell; we've traveled many miles together to see the next quilt show. Thank you to Donna Taylor for teaching me to appliqué and to the UpCountry Quilters Guild for always providing inspiration and support through the years.

Last but not least, I would like to thank Cheryl for inviting me to join her on this incredible book-writing adventure.

From Both of Us

Many thanks to AccuQuilt; Andover Fabrics, Inc.; Aurifil; BackSide Fabrics; BERNINA Sewing Center—We're in Stitches (Greenville, SC); Birch Fabrics; C&T Publishing; Cloud9 Fabrics; Cotton + Steel; Hoffman California Fabrics; Michael Miller Fabrics; Moda Fabrics; RJR Fabrics; Robert Kaufman Fabrics; Sulky of America; and The Warm Company for their generous donations of fabric, batting, thread, sewing machine rentals, and supplies.

Special thanks to Johellen George for all the wonderful longarm quilting; to Darleen Sanford for the pattern testing and reviewing; to Leslie White, owner of our local BERNINA dealership, who generously supported our book-writing efforts; and to the quilters from across the U.S. and UK who contributed a Plus block for our signature quilt.

Thank you, Stash Books, for bringing our vision to print.

Introduction   6

General Instructions   8

Fabric preparation • Abbreviations and definitions • Directional prints
Seam allowances • Pressing seams • Making half-square triangles
Fusible machine appliqué • Foundation paper piecing

CONT

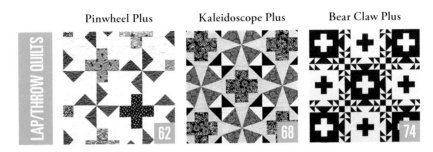

Pinwheel Plus   Kaleidoscope Plus   Bear Claw Plus

LAP/THROW QUILTS   62   68   74

ENTS

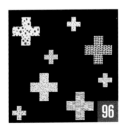

BED-SIZE QUILTS   80   84   90   96

Intertwined   Petal Plus   Transparency Chains   Celestial

introduction

Plus signs have been a universally appealing design in popular culture for over 100 years, forming some of the most recognizable logos in the world. There is no mistaking the logos of the American Red Cross and Swiss Army.

Drawn to this simple and strong geometric shape, quilters have used plus signs extensively throughout history. Some of the first popular plus sign quilt designs were signature quilts made in the early 1900s to support the Red Cross during World War I. Individuals and businesses would pay a small fee to have their name embroidered on such a quilt, and then the finished project would be raffled off to generate additional funds for the cause.

This vintage Red Cross quilt was made in Lake County, Illinois in 1915, with each resident paying 10 cents to have his or her name

embroidered on the quilt. Each of the blocks contained 1 red plus sign and about 40 embroidered names on the white background.

Photo by Mark Widhalm

Red Cross signature quilt, circa 1915, from the collections of Lake County Discovery Museum

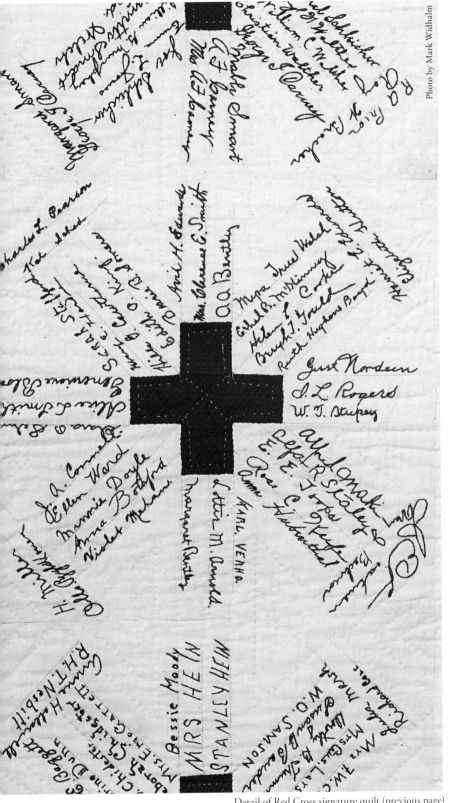

Detail of Red Cross signature quilt (previous page)

You can make your own modern version of the Red Cross signature quilt using the instructions in *Signature Plus* (page 36). Our version was made with the help of 122 quilters, each making and signing a signature block. It is the perfect pattern for a modern quilting bee.

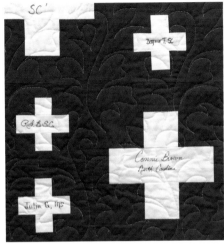

Detail of *Signature Plus* (page 36)

The plus sign's popularity in quilts has withstood the test of time, with new plus sign quilts being made every year.

This book contains sixteen different quilt patterns made with a variety of techniques, including traditional piecing, paper piecing, and appliqué. Quilt sizes range from baby through queen. A difficulty rating from "+" (most beginner friendly) to "+++" (more time consuming and challenging) is noted for each pattern.

We hope that you enjoy and are inspired by this collection of new and modern twists on the classic plus sign. We can't wait to see what you make!

general instructions

fabric preparation

An ongoing debate among quilters is whether or not to prewash fabric. Cheryl prefers the crispness from the sizing in the manufacturers' processing and usually does not prewash her fabric. Paige, on the other hand, prewashes most everything because she doesn't want any surprises from excess dyes or uneven shrinkage. When using a paper-backed fusible web for machine appliqué, manufacturers suggest prewashing your fabric. *If you prewash some of your fabric, prewash it all.*

Whether you prewash or not, be sure your fabric is pressed and free of wrinkles before you start cutting.

abbreviations and definitions

Yardages are based on fabric with a usable fabric width of 40″. The width of fabric, or *WOF*, is measured from selvage to selvage.

Using precuts is a way to include a variety of prints in your projects without purchasing a large quantity of each. Manufacturers label precuts differently, but some examples are 5″ charm squares and 10″ precut squares. Fat quarters are 18″ × 20″. Fat eighths are sometimes cut 9″ × 20″ and sometimes 10″ × 18″, so pay careful attention to the pattern requirements and how the fat eighths are packaged.

directional prints

The patterns in this book were written for nondirectional prints and include directions for cutting and piecing that make the most efficient use of the fabric. If you decide to use a directional print, such as a stripe or a group of houses, you may need additional yardage beyond what is stated in the materials list. You may also need to alter the cutting or piecing instructions. We highly recommend making a test block to see what alterations might be necessary.

seam allowances

A scant ¼″ seam allowance (a seam allowance that is a thread's width smaller than ¼″) is used for all projects in this book—except for piecing quilt backings, when a ½″ seam allowance is recommended. It is a good idea to do a test seam before you begin sewing to ensure that your scant ¼″ is accurate.

There is no need to backstitch seamlines where they will be crossed by another seam. It is helpful, however, to backstitch seams where they fall on the outer perimeter of the quilt top or backing.

pressing seams

First press the seams as sewn, right sides together. Then press the seams open or toward the darker fabric to prevent the darker fabric from showing through a lighter fabric. Both Cheryl and Paige prefer to press seams open when possible; they find that there is less distortion in the seams and the blocks lie flatter when pressed this way.

Press lightly in an up-and-down motion. Be especially careful when pressing bias edges, as they stretch easily.

With planning, seams in some blocks can be pressed in the opposite direction to the seams of adjacent fabric pieces or blocks, allowing the seams to nest together. The seams almost lock together, allowing for greater speed and accuracy in piecing.

++

making half-square triangles

Refer to the project instructions for the size of the squares.

1. With right sides together, pair 2 squares. Lightly draw a diagonal line on the wrong side of the lighter square.

Draw line.

2. Sew a scant ¼″ seam on each side of the line.

Sew.

3. Cut on the drawn line.

4. Press open and trim to size.

++

fusible machine appliqué

Appliqué projects in this book use raw-edge fusible appliqué secured with a zigzag satin stitch. Choose the width and length of the zigzag satin stitch you prefer to use.

For an alternative raw-edge finish, use a straight stitch along the outside edges of the appliqué shapes. Other techniques such as needle-turn appliqué may also be used, but be sure to add a turn-under allowance to the appliqué patterns.

Using a lightweight paper-backed fusible web such as SoftFuse Premium (available from Shades Textiles) will reduce bulk in your finished project. The key to successful appliqué is practicing on a sample first.

Preparing and Fusing Appliqué Shapes

1. Transfer the appliqué patterns onto the paper-backed fusible web using 1 of the following 3 methods. Since the appliqué patterns in *Cute as a Button* (page 26) and *Petal Plus* (page 84) are symmetrical, it is not necessary to reverse the images.

Method A: Place the paper-backed fusible web over the appliqué pattern. Trace the design onto the smooth (paper) side of the fusible web the number of times required by the instructions, leaving at least a ½″ space between the appliqué shapes.

Method B: To create repetitive shapes with greater accuracy, trace the appliqué pattern onto translucent template plastic and carefully cut out the shape using craft scissors. Trace around the plastic template onto the smooth (paper) side of the fusible web the number of times required by the instructions, leaving at least a ½″ space between the appliqué shapes.

Method C: Use a fabric cutting system such as AccuQuilt GO! dies (accuquilt.com) to create the appliqué shapes in a fraction of the time. Apply fusible web to the back of the fabric before cutting the shapes. Skip to Step 5 if using this cutting method.

2. Roughly cut out the appliqué shapes, leaving between ⅛″ to ¼″ of fusible beyond the traced line.

3. Fuse the shapes to the wrong side of your appliqué fabric following the heat settings suggested by the manufacturer.

4. Cut out the appliqué shapes on the traced lines, and remove the paper backing.

5. Position the appliqué shapes onto your background fabric squares, and fuse in place following the heat settings suggested by the manufacturer.

6. Cut iron-on tear-away stabilizer a little bigger than your appliqué shape, and iron it to the back of your background fabric according to the manufacturer's recommendations.

+++

Preparing Your Machine for Appliqué

The following machine settings and adjustments contribute to creating beautiful appliqué stitches.

+ Set your machine for a zigzag satin stitch with a width of 2–3 mm and a length of 0.35–0.5 mm.

+ Reduce the machine's top thread tension to ensure the bobbin thread does not show through on the top.

+ Switch the presser foot to an open-toe embroidery foot for better visibility.

+ Set your machine to needle down if it has the capability. This will aid in stitching smooth curves.

+ Fill your bobbin with a fine 60-weight polyester or bobbin thread.

+ Change to a new sharp needle compatible with your thread and fabric choices.

Stitching the Appliqué Shapes

1. Start stitching into the background fabric with your needle in the down position on the right and just beyond the appliqué shape. Keep the thread tails long and out of the way. The zigzag satin stitch should cover the raw edge of your appliqué shape, and the needle should enter the background fabric very close to the edge of the appliqué shape without fraying it.

2. Stitch slowly, and strive for evenly spaced stitches perpendicular to the edge of your appliqué shape.

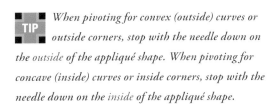

TIP *When pivoting for convex (outside) curves or outside corners, stop with the needle down on the outside of the appliqué shape. When pivoting for concave (inside) curves or inside corners, stop with the needle down on the inside of the appliqué shape.*

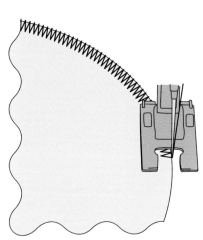

Needle enters background fabric very close to appliqué shape; note that appliqué is visible using open-toe foot.

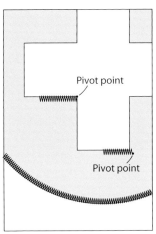

Pivot points for inside and outside corners

✚✚✚

3. Stop about ½″ before your starting point, lift your presser foot, and adjust the beginning thread tail to stitch right over it with the remaining stitches. This avoids the need to bury the thread.

4. Stop stitching when you reach the beginning point. Again, leave long thread tails.

5. Snip the loose end of the beginning needle thread that has been anchored under the stitching. Pull the ending needle thread to the back by gently pulling

the bobbin thread; a small loop of the needle thread will appear. Tie the loose threads together, and use a needle to bury them under the channel formed by the zigzag satin stitch.

6. Gently tear away the stabilizer, supporting the stitches as you tear.

7. Square up the blocks according to the pattern instructions, using your rotary mat and ruler.

foundation paper piecing

Paper piecing is a precise stitching method in which perfect points and nonstandard angles can be achieved that would otherwise be challenging with traditional piecing. The stitching is done in numerical order on the printed side of the foundation, with the fabric placed on the unprinted side of the foundation. The finished unit will be a mirror image of the printed pattern.

TIP *In paper piecing, each quilter has a different preference on the size of the fabric piece relative to the size of the paper-pieced block section. We strongly recommend that you first make one of each paper-pieced block before cutting large numbers of fabric pieces to see if the fabric sizes listed fit into your comfort zone.*

Preparing Paper-Piecing Patterns

1. Copy each foundation (pages 105–109) the number of times required by the quilt pattern onto standard copy paper or foundation paper, such as Carol Doak's Foundation Paper (by C&T Publishing). *It is always a good idea to make 1 or 2 extra foundations in case of mistakes.*

2. Trim the printed foundation paper, leaving a ½″ margin outside the outer lines.

Paper Piecing

1. Reduce the machine's stitch length to around 1.5 mm or 18 stitches per inch, and use a size 90/14 needle to make paper removal easier after the block is sewn.

2. Crease the seamline between segments 1 and 2 on the foundation paper. A piece of template plastic or a straightedge will aid in folding the paper accurately on what will be your first stitching line.

3. Place the fabrics for segments 1 and 2 right sides together on the *unprinted side* of the paper, oriented such that the wrong side of fabric 1 is touching the paper and extends beyond segment 1 at least ¼″ all around. The edges of fabrics 1 and 2 should be parallel to the crease made in Step 2 and overhang by at least ¼″. Audition fabric placement by holding the foundation paper up to a light source to be certain that segment 1 is covered and that once it is sewn and pressed, segment 2 will be completely covered by fabric 2. Pin in place.

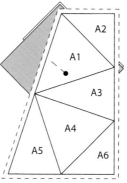

Printed side of foundation paper

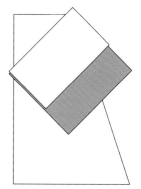

Unprinted side of foundation paper

4. Orient the foundation paper so the printed side is facing up and the fabrics are on the unprinted side of the paper. Sew on the printed seamline between segments 1 and 2. (Stitches are shown in red on the illustration for visibility.)

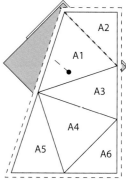

Sew on printed seamline.

5. Fold the paper again along the stitched line, and trim the seam allowance to ¼″.

6. Open and press fabric 2 in place using a dry iron.

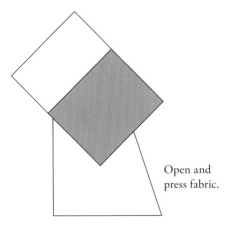

Open and press fabric.

7. With the foundation paper *printed* side up, crease the seamline between segments 1 and 3 as you did in Step 2 (previous page). After the fold is made, the wrong side of fabric 1 should be visible and extend at least ¼″. Using your ruler and rotary cutter, trim the seam allowance to ¼″.

8. Turn the foundation paper to the *unprinted* side. Align fabric 3 right sides together with fabric 1, testing to make sure fabric 3 will cover area 3, as you did in Step 3 (previous page).

9. Repeat Steps 4–8 in the same manner with fabric 3, and continue with the remaining fabrics in numerical order until the foundation is completely sewn.

10. Trim the block along the foundation's outer lines, leaving the ¼″ seam allowances intact.

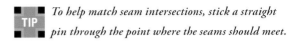 *Because you will be cutting through both fabric and paper when trimming foundations, it is best to have a dedicated rotary cutter and blade for paper so that you do not dull your blade for fabric cutting.*

Sewing Together Paper-Pieced Units

1. Align the paper-pieced units together, matching the seams.

To help match seam intersections, stick a straight pin through the point where the seams should meet.

2. Sew the units together, aligning the edges. Press the seams open, as most paper-pieced blocks have bulky seams.

When sewing units together, baste the seam first using a basting stitch (2.8–3.5 mm), check seam alignment, and then sew again using the regular stitch length. This makes it easier to unsew, if need be.

3. Remove the foundation paper. The paper can be removed as soon as the blocks are complete, or you can wait until the quilt top is finished. We recommend removing the paper from the completed seams after each seam is sewn.

rick rack runner

Designed, pieced, and quilted
by Paige Alexander

Rick Rack Runner uses rows of plus signs to make a versatile bed or table runner. This runner is a great way to utilize some precut or scrap fabrics, and the length can be resized easily to suit your needs.

Materials

Yardages are based on fabric that is 40″ wide.

Prints: 13 precut 10″ × 10″ squares

Ivory: 1⅝ yards

Binding: ½ yard

Batting: 31″ × 95″

Backing: 2⅝ yards

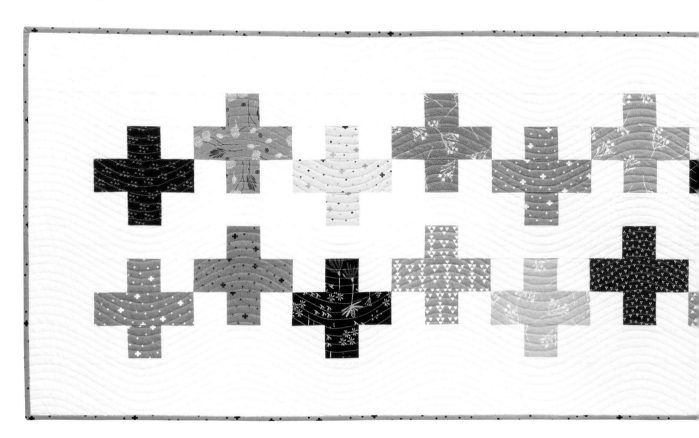

finished block	finished quilt	difficulty
6″ × 8″	22½″ × 86½″	+

Cutting

PRINTS

From *each* 10″ precut square, cut 2 rectangles 2½″ × 6½″ and 4 squares 2½″ × 2½″.

IVORY

Cut 1 strip 4½″ × width of fabric (WOF).

+ Subcut into 2 rectangles 4½″ × 16½″.

Cut 5 strips 3½″ × WOF.

+ Subcut 1 strip into 2 rectangles 3½″ × 20″.

Cut 12 strips 2½″ × WOF.

+ Subcut 5 strips into 26 rectangles 2½″ × 6½″; each strip yields 6 rectangles.

+ Subcut 7 strips into 104 squares 2½″ × 2½″; each strip yields 16 squares.

BINDING

Cut 6 strips 2½″ × WOF.

Fabric: Desert Bloom by Sherri & Chelsi for Moda Fabrics

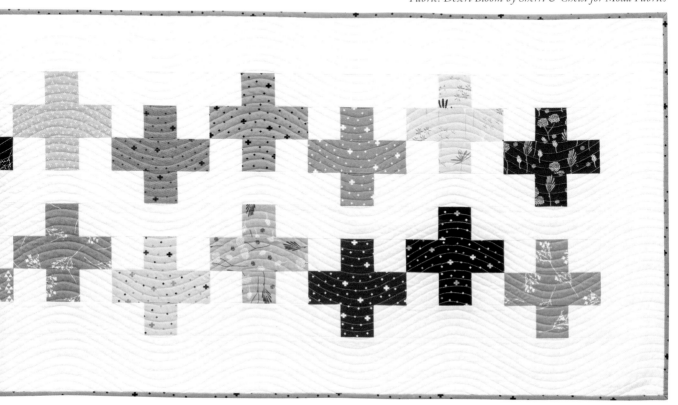

instructions

Seam allowances are a scant ¼" unless otherwise noted. Press all seams open unless otherwise noted.

Block Assembly

 Use matching print fabric pieces within each block.

1. Sew together a print 2½" square and 2 ivory 2½" squares, pressing the seams toward the print square. Repeat to make a total of 52 units.

2. Sew together an ivory 2½" × 6½" rectangle, 2 units from Step 1, and a print 2½" × 6½" rectangle, pressing the seams toward the ivory and print rectangles. The block should measure 6½" × 8½". Repeat to make a total of 26 blocks.

Block assembly

Quilt Top Assembly

1. Arrange the blocks in a 13 × 2 arrangement, rotating the blocks to match the quilt top assembly diagram (below). Make sure the colors and patterns within the blocks are arranged in a pleasing manner.

2. Sew the blocks into rows, and sew the rows together to make the quilt top. The quilt top should measure 16½" × 78½" before the borders are added.

Borders

1. Sew the ivory 4½" × 16½" rectangles to the sides of the quilt top.

2. Sew 2 ivory 3½" × WOF strips and 1 ivory 3½" × 20" rectangle together end to end. Repeat to make a total of 2 pieced top/bottom borders.

3. Measure the average width of the quilt top, and trim the 2 top/bottom borders to fit (approximately 86½"). Sew the top and bottom borders to the quilt top.

Finishing

Refer to Finishing Your Quilt (page 100) as needed.

1. To make the quilt back, cut the backing fabric into 3 pieces each 31" × WOF, trim off the selvage edges, and sew the pieces together along the trimmed selvage edges. Trim the backing to approximately 31" × 95".

2. Layer the quilt top, batting, and backing. Baste and quilt as desired. Bind and enjoy! This version of Rick Rack Runner was quilted in an echoed wavy-line pattern.

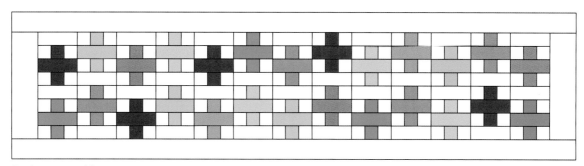

Quilt top assembly

row addition

Designed, pieced, and quilted
by Cheryl Brickey

*Using just five solid fabrics and a "plus" fabric, this baby-size quilt comes
together quickly and easily. The design would also look great in large-
scale prints instead of solid fabrics.*

Materials

*Yardages are based on
fabric that is 40" wide.*

White: ¼ yard

Color fabrics: ½ yard
each of 5 fabrics

Binding: ½ yard

Batting: 49" × 54"

Backing: 2¾ yards

Cutting

WHITE

Cut 2 strips
2½" × width of
fabric (WOF).

+ Subcut 1 strip
  into 5 rectangles
  2½" × 6½".

+ Subcut 1 strip
  into 10 squares
  2½" × 2½".

COLOR FABRICS

Cut the following
pieces from *each*
color according to the
cutting diagram:

+ 1 rectangle
  24" × 9½"

+ 1 rectangle 8" × 9½"

+ 4 squares 4" × 4"

+ 4 rectangles 2" × 2½"

BINDING

Cut 5 strips
2½" × WOF.

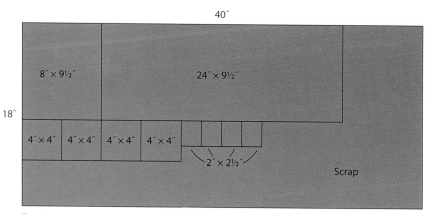

Cutting

finished block	finished quilt	difficulty
9″ × 9″	40½″ × 45½″	+

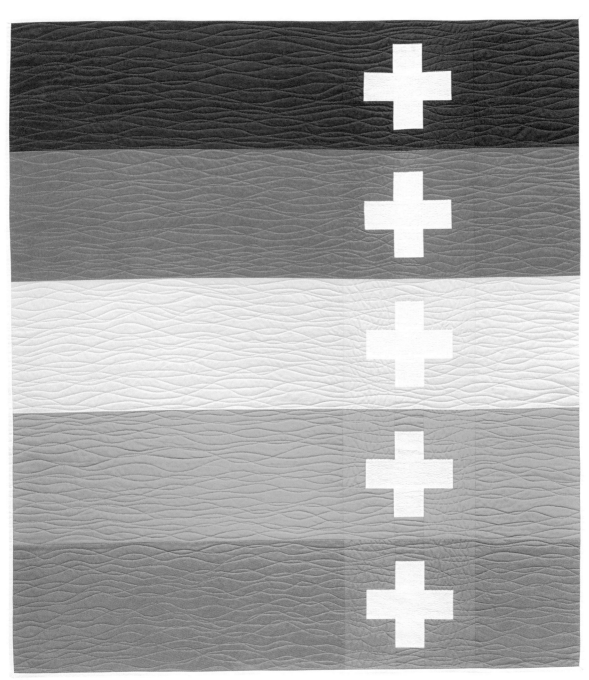

Fabric: Cotton Supreme Solids by RJR Studio for RJR Fabrics

instructions

Seam allowances are a scant ¼″ unless otherwise noted. Press all seams open unless otherwise noted.

Block Assembly

 TIP *Use the same-color pieces within each Plus block.*

1. Sew a white 2½″ square to a color 2″ × 2½″ rectangle to make a unit. Repeat to make a total of 2 units.

2. Sew a unit from Step 1 between 2 color 4″ squares. Repeat with the second unit.

3. Sew a white 2½″ × 6½″ rectangle between 2 color 2″ × 2½″ rectangles.

4. Sew the rows together to make 1 Plus block. The block should measure 9½″ × 9½″. Repeat to make a total of 5 Plus blocks.

Plus block assembly

Quilt Top Assembly

1. Sew together the following pieces and a Plus block of the same color according to the row assembly diagram. The row should measure 9½″ × 40½″.

+ 1 rectangle 9½″ × 24″

+ 1 Plus block

+ 1 rectangle 9½″ × 8″

Repeat to make a total of 5 rows.

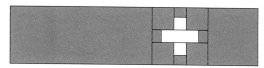

Row assembly

2. Arrange the rows according to the quilt top assembly diagram.

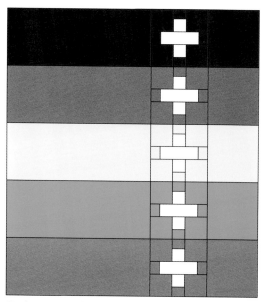

Quilt top assembly

3. Sew the rows together to make the quilt top, which should measure 40½″ × 45½″.

Finishing

Refer to Finishing Your Quilt (page 100) as needed.

1. To make the quilt back, cut the backing fabric into 2 pieces each 49″ × WOF, trim off the selvage edges, and sew the pieces together along the trimmed selvage edges. Trim to approximately 49″ × 54″.

2. Layer the quilt top, batting, and backing. Baste and quilt as desired. Bind and enjoy! This version of *Row Addition* was quilted in an overlapping wave pattern in the rows and a dense back-and-forth design in the plus signs.

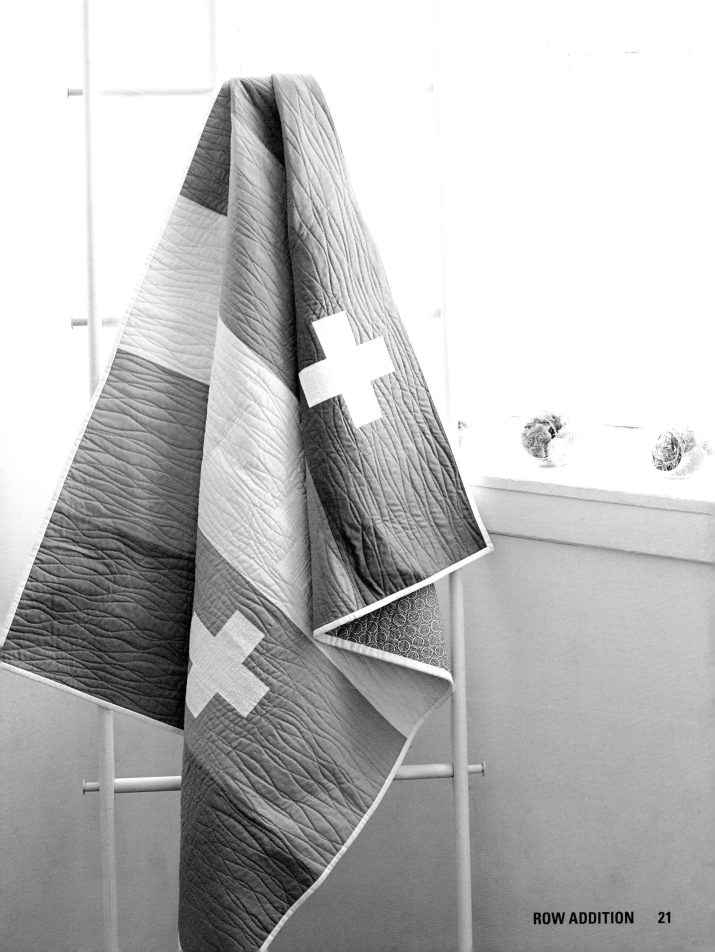

message in a bottle

Designed, pieced, and quilted by Cheryl Brickey

Message in a Bottle *has a strong geometric pattern with the oversized and outlined plus sign. It is a perfect baby quilt when you want a striking design that is quick and simple to make. You can scale* Message in a Bottle *into a queen-size quilt easily by making four baby-size quilts and sewing them together in a 2 × 2 arrangement.*

Materials

Yardages are based on fabric that is 40″ wide.

Red: ½ yard

Blue: ⅝ yard

Gray: 1¾ yards

Binding: ½ yard

Batting: 57″ × 57″

Backing: 3¼ yards

Cutting

RED

Cut 4 strips 3½″ × width of fabric (WOF).

+ Subcut into 4 rectangles 3½″ × 11½″, 4 rectangles 3½″ × 10½″, and 4 rectangles 3½″ × 8½″; each strip yields 1 rectangle of each size.

BLUE

Cut the following pieces according to the cutting diagram:

+ 1 rectangle 10½″ × 16½″

+ 2 rectangles 8½″ × 10½″

+ 2 rectangles 10½″ × 5½″

GRAY

Cut 2 strips 16½″ × WOF.

+ Subcut into 4 squares 16½″ × 16½″; each strip yields 2 squares.

Cut 2 strips 8½″ × WOF.

+ Subcut into 4 rectangles 8½″ × 16½″; each strip yields 2 rectangles.

BINDING

Cut 6 strips 2½″ × WOF.

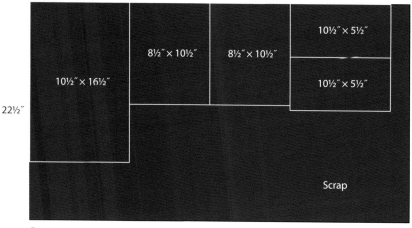

40″

22½″

10½″ × 16½″

8½″ × 10½″

8½″ × 10½″

10½″ × 5½″

10½″ × 5½″

Scrap

Cutting

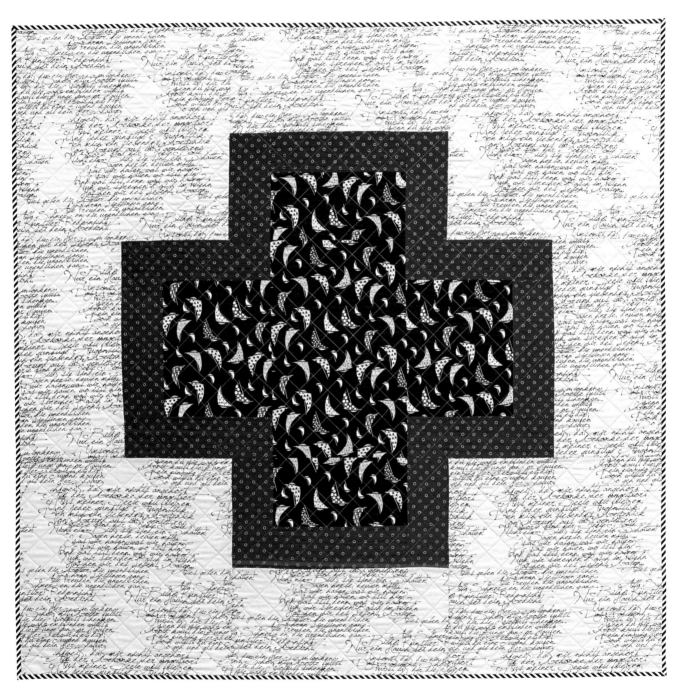

Fabrics: Daysail and Hello Darling by Bonnie & Camille and Modern Background Paper by Zen Chic—all for Moda Fabrics

instructions

Seam allowances are a scant ¼" unless otherwise noted. Press all seams open unless otherwise noted.

First Units

1. Sew together a red 3½" × 10½" rectangle and a blue 5½" × 10½" rectangle.

2. Sew together the unit from Step 1 and 2 red 3½" × 8½" rectangles to make a unit measuring 8½" × 16½".

3. Sew together the unit from Step 2 and 1 gray 8½" × 16½" rectangle to make a first unit measuring 16½" × 16½". Repeat to make 2 first units.

First unit assembly

Second Units

1. Sew together a red 3½" × 10½" rectangle and a blue 8½" × 10½" rectangle.

2. Sew together the unit from Step 1 and 2 red 3½" × 11½" rectangles to make a unit measuring 11½" × 16½".

3. Sew together the unit from Step 2 and 1 gray 8½" × 16½" rectangle to make a second unit measuring 16½" × 19½". Repeat to make 2 second units.

Second unit assembly

Quilt Top Assembly

1. Arrange and rotate the following according to the quilt top assembly diagram (above right).

+ 2 first units

+ 2 second units

+ 4 gray squares 16½" × 16½"

+ 1 blue rectangle 10½" × 16½"

2. Sew into 3 rows. Sew the rows together to make the quilt top, which should measure 48½" × 48½".

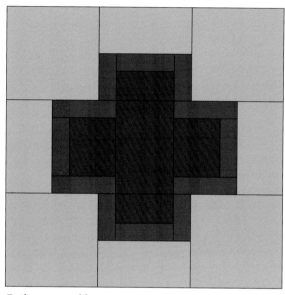

Quilt top assembly

Finishing

Refer to Finishing Your Quilt (page 100) as needed.

1. To make the quilt back, cut the backing fabric into 2 pieces each 57" × WOF, trim off the selvage edges, and sew the pieces together along the trimmed selvage edges. Trim to approximately 57" × 57".

2. Layer the quilt top, batting, and backing. Baste and quilt as desired. Bind and enjoy! This version of *Message in a Bottle* was quilted in a crosshatch pattern.

cute as a button

Designed, pieced, and quilted
by Paige Alexander

*Nesting plus signs within circles made from colorful fabrics creates fun
motifs resembling buttons appliquéd onto background squares.*

Materials

Yardages are based on fabric that is 40″ wide.

Appliqué: 1 charm square pack (or 36 squares 5″ × 5″)

Background: 2 yards

Binding: ½ yard

Batting: 48″ × 48″

Backing: 2⅔ yards

Paper-backed fusible web: 36 squares 5″ × 5″

Iron-on tear-away stabilizer: 36 squares 5½″ × 5½″

Cutting

BACKGROUND

**Cut 8 strips 7″ × width
of fabric (WOF).**

+ Subcut into
  36 squares 7″ × 7″;
  each strip yields
  5 squares.

Cut 4 strips 2″ × WOF.

BINDING

**Cut 5 strips
2½″ × WOF.**

finished block	finished quilt	difficulty
6" × 6"	39½" × 39½"	

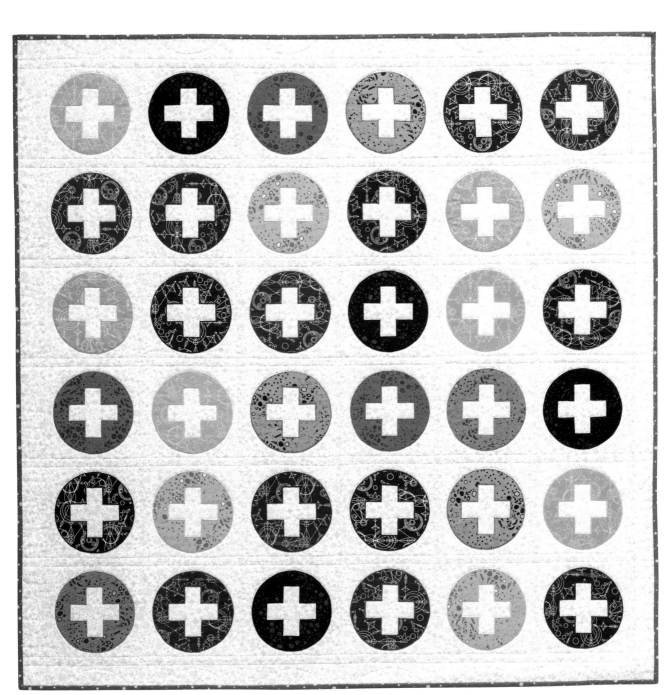

Fabrics: Sun Print 2015 and Sun Print 2016 by Alison Glass for Andover Fabrics, Inc.

instructions

See Fusible Machine Appliqué (page 9) to appliqué the blocks.

Block Assembly

1. Create 36 appliqué shapes using the *Cute As a Button* circle plus pattern (page 104), the appliqué fabric squares, and the paper-backed fusible web.

2. Center and fuse the appliqué shapes onto the background squares.

3. Center and iron the stabilizer onto the back of the background squares.

4. Using a zigzag satin stitch or your desired stitch, appliqué around the outside and inside of the 36 circle plus appliqué shapes. Carefully remove the stabilizer from the blocks.

 TIP *A 6½″ × 6½″ ruler can be used to quickly square up the blocks.*

5. Trim the Plus blocks to 6½″ × 6½″.

Plus block

Quilt Top Assembly

Seam allowances are a scant ¼″ unless otherwise noted. Press all seams open unless otherwise noted.

1. Arrange the Plus blocks in a 6 × 6 arrangement according to the quilt top assembly diagram (at right).

2. Sew the blocks into rows. Sew the rows together to make the quilt top, which should measure 36½″ × 36½″ before the borders are added.

Borders

1. Measure the average height of the quilt top, and trim 2 background 2″ × WOF strips to fit (approximately 36½″). Attach the side borders to the quilt top.

2. Measure the average width of the quilt top, and trim 2 background 2″ × WOF strips to fit (approximately 39½″). Attach the top and bottom borders to the quilt top.

Finishing

Refer to Finishing Your Quilt (page 100) as needed.

1. To make the quilt back, cut the 2⅔ yards into 2 pieces each 48″ × WOF, trim off the selvage edges, and sew the pieces together along the trimmed selvage edges. Trim to approximately 48″ × 48″.

2. Layer the quilt top, batting, and backing. Baste and quilt as desired. Bind and enjoy! This version of *Cute As a Button* was quilted by outlining the inside and outside of the appliqué shapes and with straight lines echoing the block seamlines.

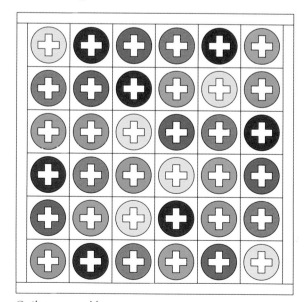

Quilt top assembly

faceted rings

Designed, pieced, and quilted
by Cheryl Brickey

Faceted Rings *uses foundation paper piecing to create interesting angles and a ring shape surrounding the plus signs. This quilt could easily be scaled up to a lap or bed quilt by adding more blocks.*

Materials

Yardages are based on fabric that is 40″ wide.

Light purple: ⅜ yard

White: 1⅜ yards

Dark gray: ½ yard

Yellow: 1⅜ yards

Dark purple: ½ yard

Light gray: ½ yard

Binding: ½ yard

Batting: 48″ × 48″

Backing: 2⅔ yards

Foundation paper: 72 sheets 8½″ × 11″

Cutting

TIP *Each quilter has a different preference on the size of the fabric piece relative to the size of the paper-pieced block section. It is highly recommended that you first make one block before cutting large numbers of fabric pieces to see if the fabric sizes listed fit into your comfort zone.*

LIGHT PURPLE

Cut 4 strips 2½″ × width of fabric (WOF).

+ Subcut the strips into 36 rectangles 2½″ × 4″; each strip yields 10 rectangles.

WHITE

Cut 9 strips 3¼″ × WOF.

+ Subcut into 72 rectangles 3¼″ × 5″; each strip yields 8 rectangles.

Cut 5 strips 2½″ × WOF.

+ Subcut into 72 squares 2½″ × 2½″; each strip yields 16 squares.

DARK GRAY

Cut 6 strips 2¼″ × WOF.

+ Subcut into 36 rectangles 2¼″ × 6″; each strip yields 6 rectangles.

YELLOW

Cut 11 strips 3″ × WOF.

+ Subcut into 72 rectangles 3″ × 5½″; each strip yields 7 rectangles.

Cut 4 strips 2¼″ × WOF.

DARK PURPLE

Cut 4 strips 2½″ × WOF.

+ Subcut into 36 rectangles 2½″ × 4″; each strip yields 10 rectangles.

LIGHT GRAY

Cut 6 strips 2¼″ × WOF.

+ Subcut into 36 rectangles 2¼″ × 6″; each strip yields 6 rectangles.

BINDING

Cut 5 strips 2½″ × WOF.

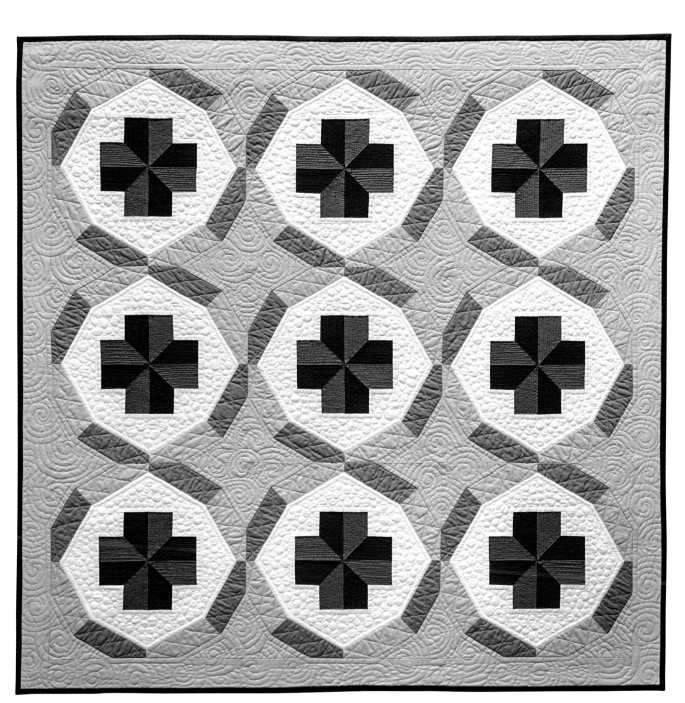

Fabric: Kona Cotton solids by Robert Kaufman Fabrics in Ash, Geranium, Gumdrop, Smoke, Wasabi, and White

instructions

Use the foundation paper-piecing directions (page 12) to sew the paper-pieced blocks.

Block Assembly

1. Trace or photocopy *Faceted Rings* foundation patterns A and B onto foundation paper the number of times indicated.

2. Paper piece each foundation using the following precut pieces:

Faceted Rings Foundation A

Use foundation A (page 105); make 36.

Segment A1	Light purple rectangle 2½″ × 4″
Segment A2	White square 2½″ × 2½″
Segment A3	White rectangle 3¼″ × 5″
Segment A4	Dark gray rectangle 2¼″ × 6″
Segment A5	Yellow rectangle 3″ × 5½″

Faceted Rings Foundation B

Use foundation B (page 106); make 36.

Segment B1	Dark purple rectangle 2½″ × 4″
Segment B2	White square 2½″ × 2½″
Segment B3	White rectangle 3¼″ × 5″
Segment B4	Light gray rectangle 2¼″ × 6″
Segment B5	Yellow rectangle 3″ × 5½″

3. Trim each unit along the foundation's outer seam allowance lines.

4. Sew foundations A and B together to make a unit measuring 6½″ × 6½″. Repeat to make 36 units.

Unit assembly

5. Sew 4 units together to make a block measuring 12½″ × 12½″. Repeat to make a total of 9 blocks.

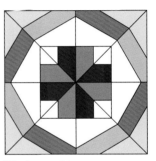

Block assembly

Quilt Top Assembly

Seam allowances are a scant ¼″ unless otherwise noted. Press all seams open unless otherwise noted.

1. Arrange the blocks in a 3 × 3 arrangement according to the quilt top assembly diagram.

2. Sew the blocks into rows. Sew the rows together to make the quilt top, which should measure 36½″ × 36½″ before the borders are added.

Quilt top assembly

Borders

1. Measure the average height of the quilt top, and trim 2 yellow strips 2¼″ × WOF to fit (approximately 36½″). Attach the side borders to the quilt top.

2. Measure the average width of the quilt top, and trim 2 yellow strips 2¼″ × WOF to fit (approximately 40″). Attach the top and bottom borders to the quilt top.

Finishing

Refer to Finishing Your Quilt (page 100) as needed.

1. To make the quilt back, cut the 2⅔ yards into 2 pieces each 48″ × WOF, trim off the selvage edges, and sew the pieces together along the trimmed selvage edges. Trim to approximately 48″ × 48″.

2. Layer the quilt top, batting, and backing. Baste and quilt as desired. Bind and enjoy! This version of *Faceted Rings* was quilted using dense back-and-forth patterns in the plus signs, pebbles in the white areas, a crosshatch in the circle areas, and swirls in the yellow areas.

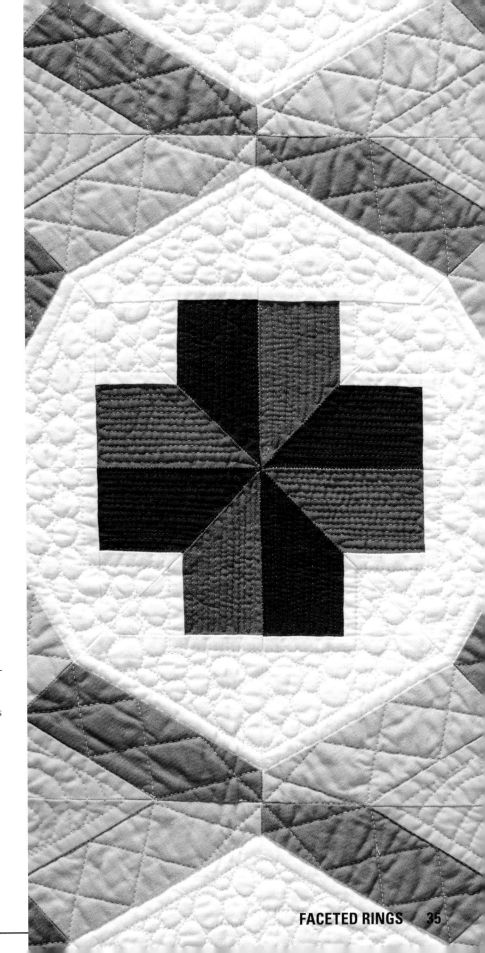

signature plus

Designed and assembled by Cheryl Brickey
and quilted by Johellen George

Red Cross signature block quilts were used in the early twentieth century to fund the Red Cross during World War I. Typically, there was a donation required to have the quilter embroider the donor's name or business onto a block, and the finished quilt would be auctioned off to raise more money. This signature quilt is a modern version of the classic Red Cross quilt. It was made from quilt blocks donated by quilters, each of whom signed their name and location.

Materials

Yardages are based on fabric that is 40″ wide.

 TIP *You may wish to purchase additional yardage or extra fabric pieces to account for some of the blocks not being completed or returned by group members.*

Red: 7¼ yards *or* 40 large fabric pieces 10″ × 12″, 10 fabric pieces 2¾″ × 9½″, and 82 small fabric pieces 7″ × 7″

White: 2⅝ yards *or* 40 large fabric pieces 6″ × 8″ and 82 small fabric pieces 4″ × 4″

Binding: ⅔ yard

Batting: 72″ × 90″

Backing: 5 yards

Fabric Preparation

Use this cutting list if starting with yardage of red and white fabrics.

RED

Cut 10 strips 12″ × width of fabric (WOF).

+ Subcut into 40 large pieces 12″ × 10″; each strip yields 4 large pieces.

Cut 17 strips 7″ × WOF.

+ Subcut into 82 small pieces 7″ × 7″; each strip yields 5 small pieces.

Cut 3 strips 2¾″ × WOF.

+ Subcut into 10 rectangles 2¾″ × 9½″; each strip yields 4 rectangles.

WHITE

Cut 8 strips 6″ × WOF.

+ Subcut into 40 large pieces 6″ × 8″; each strip yields 5 large pieces.

Cut 9 strips 4″ × WOF.

+ Subcut into 82 small pieces 4″ × 4″; each strip yields 10 small pieces.

BINDING

Cut 8 strips 2½″ × WOF.

finished blocks	finished quilt	difficulty
4½" × 4½" and 9" × 9"	63½" × 81½"	✚

Fabric: Cotton Couture by Michael Miller Fabrics in Bright White and Cherry

Signature Plus *is well suited for group quilts, as the blocks can be made oversize and then trimmed down.*

To make Signature Plus, *you can distribute fabric to your quilting friends or sewing-bee mates in order to have all the same fabrics in the quilt, or you can have each quilter use their own fabrics for a scrappier look.*

instructions for group block makers

oversized blocks

Seam allowances are a scant ¼″ unless otherwise noted. Press all seams open unless otherwise noted.

Have quilters make a total of 40 large and 82 small Plus blocks.

Cutting

FOR EACH LARGE PLUS BLOCK

Cut 4 (A) squares 4¼″ × 4¼″ and 4 (B) rectangles 2¼″ × 2½″ from 1 large red fabric portion.

Cut 1 (C) rectangle 2½″ × 6½″ and 2 (D) squares 2½″ × 2½″ from 1 large white fabric portion.

FOR EACH SMALL PLUS BLOCK

Cut 4 (A) squares 2½″ × 2½″ and 4 (B) squares 1½″ × 1½″ from 1 small red fabric portion.

Cut 1 (C) rectangle 1½″ × 3½″ and 2 (D) squares 1½″ × 1½″ from 1 small white fabric portion.

Block Assembly

1. Sew 1 D square and 1 B piece together to make a unit. Repeat to make a total of 2 units.

2. Sew each unit from Step 1 between 2 A squares.

3. Sew 1 C rectangle between 2 B pieces.

4. Sew the rows together to make a large or small Plus block. A large Plus block should measure 10″ × 10″, and a small Plus block should measure 5½″ × 5½″.

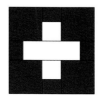

Large and small
Plus block assembly

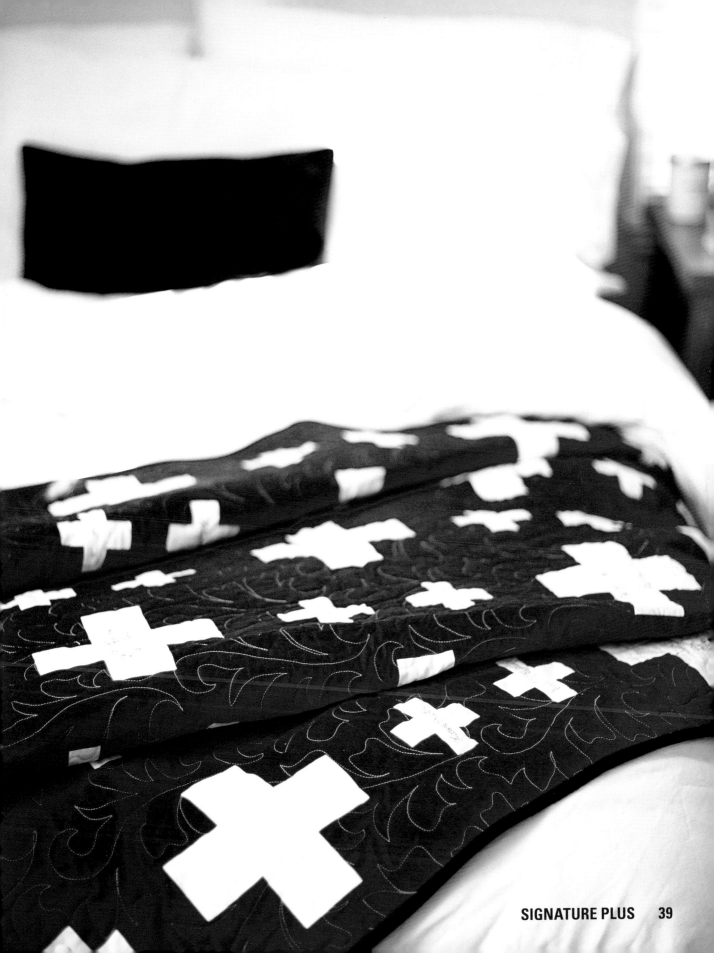

instructions for individual block makers

actual-size blocks

If you are making this quilt yourself instead of as a group or bee quilt,
you can make the Plus blocks actual size instead of oversizing and then trimming.

Cutting

FOR EACH LARGE PLUS BLOCK

Cut 4 (A) squares 4″ × 4″ and 4 (B) rectangles
2″ × 2½″ from 1 large red fabric portion.

Cut 1 (C) rectangle 2½″ × 6½″ and 2 (D) squares
2½″ × 2½″ from 1 large white fabric portion.

FOR EACH SMALL PLUS BLOCK

Cut 4 (A) squares 2¼″ × 2¼″ and 4 (B) rectangles
1¼″ × 1½″ from 1 small red fabric portion.

Cut 1 (C) rectangle 1½″ × 3½″ and 2 (D) squares
1½″ × 1½″ from 1 small white fabric portion.

Block Assembly

1. Sew 1 D square and 1 B square together to make
a unit. Repeat to make a total of 2 units.

2. Sew each unit from Step 1 between 2 A squares.

3. Sew 1 C rectangle between 2 B squares.

4. Sew the rows together
to make a large or small Plus
block. A large Plus block
should measure 9½″ × 9½″,
and a small Plus block should
measure 5″ × 5″.

Large and small
Plus block assembly

+++

Quilt Top Assembly

1. Trim each large block to 9½″ × 9½″ and each small block to 5″ × 5″, if necessary.

2. Sew the small blocks together into 41 pairs.

3. Sew together 5 pairs of small blocks, 4 large blocks, and 2 red 2¾″ × 9½″ rectangles to make 1 row A.
Repeat to make 5 rows A.

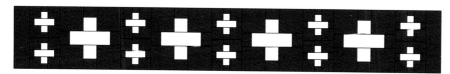

Row A
assembly

4. Sew together 5 large blocks and 4 pairs of small blocks to make 1 row B. Repeat to make 4 rows B.

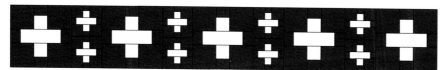

Row B
assembly

5. Sew the rows together to make the quilt top, which should measure 63½″ × 81½″.

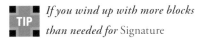 *If you wind up with more blocks than needed for* Signature Plus, *you can use them to make a table runner, pillow, or mini quilt, as shown.*

Quilt top assembly

Finishing

Refer to Finishing Your Quilt (page 100) as needed.

1. To make the quilt back, cut the backing fabric into 2 pieces each 90″ × WOF, trim off the selvage edges, and sew the pieces together along the trimmed selvage edges. Trim to approximately 72″ × 90″.

2. Layer the quilt top, batting, and backing. Baste and quilt as desired. Bind and enjoy! This version of *Signature Plus* was quilted in an overall leaf pattern.

postage plus

Designed, pieced, and quilted
by Cheryl Brickey

Postage Plus *is a great design to use with your favorite precut
fabric strips or a scrappy stack of 2½″ squares.*

Materials

Yardages are based on fabric that is 40″ wide.

Green/blue fabrics: 24 strips 2½″ × 21″ *or*
192 squares 2½″ × 2½″

Gray: 1¾ yards

White: 1½ yards

Binding: ⅝ yard

Batting: 63″ × 81″

Backing: 4½ yards

Cutting

GRAY

Cut 6 strips 8½″ × width of fabric (WOF).

+ Subcut 1 strip into 2 rectangles 8½″ × 20″.

+ Subcut 2 strips into 4 rectangles 8½″ × 19½″;
  each strip yields 2 rectangles.

+ Subcut 1 strip into 2 rectangles 8½″ × 11½″
  and 4 rectangles 8½″ × 4½″.

WHITE

Cut 5 strips 8½″ × WOF.

+ Subcut 1 strip into 2 rectangles 8½″ × 20″.

+ Subcut 1 strip into 3 rectangles 8½″ × 11½″.

+ Subcut 1 strip into 1 rectangle 8½″ × 11½″
  and 4 rectangles 8½″ × 4½″.

BINDING

Cut 7 strips 2½″ × WOF.

finished quilt
54½″ × 72½″

difficulty

*Fabrics: Essex Yarn Dyed linen in Black and Kona Cotton solids in assorted
blues and greens—both by Robert Kaufman Fabrics*

instructions

Seam allowances are a scant ¼″ unless otherwise noted. Press all seams open unless otherwise noted.

Quad Units

If starting with green/blue strips, sew 4 green/blue strips together. Repeat to make 6 strip sets. Cut the strip sets into 48 quad units 2½″ × 8½″; each strip set yields 8 quad units.

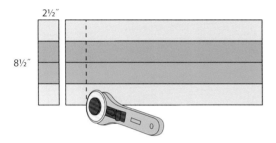

If starting with 2½″ squares, sew 4 green/blue squares together to make a quad unit measuring 2½″ × 8½″. Repeat to make 48 quad units.

Postage Stamp Blocks

 TIP *Use quad units from different strip sets, and rotate some 180° for a random scrappy look to each block.*

1. Sew 4 quad units together to make a full Postage block measuring 8½″ × 8½″. Repeat to make 8 full Postage blocks.

Full Postage block assembly

2. Sew 2 quad units and 1 gray 4½″ × 8½″ rectangle together to make a gray Postage block measuring 8½″ × 8½″. Repeat to make 4 gray Postage blocks.

Gray Postage block assembly

3. Sew 2 quad units and 1 white 4½″ × 8½″ rectangle together to make a white Postage block measuring 8½″ × 8½″. Repeat to make 4 white Postage blocks.

White Postage block assembly

+++

Quilt Top Assembly

1. Sew the strips and blocks into 9 rows as follows. Each row should measure 8½″ × 54½″.

Rows 1 and 9: Sew together 1 gray 8½″ × WOF strip and 1 gray 8½″ × 20″ rectangle end to end. Trim to 54½″ wide.

Rows 2 and 8: Sew together 1 white 8½″ × WOF strip and 1 white 8½″ × 20″ rectangle end to end. Trim to 54½″ wide.

Rows 3 and 7: Sew together 2 gray 8½″ × 19½″ rectangles and 2 gray Postage blocks.

Rows 4 and 6: Sew together 2 white 8½″ × 11½″ rectangles, 2 white Postage blocks, and 2 full Postage blocks.

Row 5: Sew together 2 gray 8½″ × 11½″ rectangles and 4 full Postage blocks.

2. Sew the rows together according to the quilt top assembly diagram. The quilt top should measure 54½″ × 72½″.

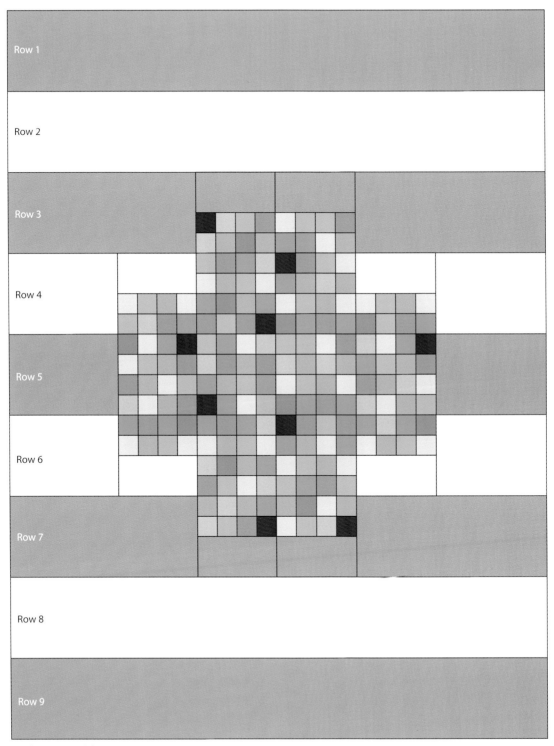

Quilt top assembly

Finishing

Refer to Finishing Your Quilt (page 100) as needed.

1. To make the quilt back, cut the backing fabric into 2 pieces each 81″ × WOF, trim off the selvage edges, and sew the pieces together along the trimmed selvage edges. Trim to approximately 63″ × 81″.

2. Layer the quilt top, batting, and backing. Baste and quilt as desired. Bind and enjoy! This version of *Postage Plus* was quilted in a combination of straight lines and a vine pattern.

plus surround

Designed, pieced, and quilted
by Paige Alexander

Plus Surround is a graphic lap-size quilt with a bull's-eye layout.
The design would pop with lighter plus signs on a darker background.

Materials

Yardages are based on fabric that is 40" wide.

Aqua: ½ yard

White: 4⅛ yards

Blue: ⅓ yard

Orange: 1 fat quarter (18" × 20")

Binding: ⅔ yard

Batting: 76" × 76"

Backing: 4¼ yards

Cutting

AQUA

Cut 4 strips 3½" × width of fabric (WOF).

+ Subcut 2 strips into 8 rectangles 3½" × 9½"; each strip yields 4 rectangles.

WHITE

Cut 5 strips 14" × WOF.

+ Subcut 2 strips into 4 squares 14" × 14" and 4 rectangles 14" × 5"; each strip yields 2 squares and 2 rectangles.

+ Subcut 2 strips into 8 rectangles 14" × 8¾"; each strip yields 4 rectangles.

+ Subcut 1 strip into 4 rectangles 14" × 6½" and 4 rectangles 14" × 3½".

Cut 2 strips 5¾" × WOF.

+ Subcut into 8 rectangles 5¾" × 8¾"; each strip yields 4 rectangles.

Cut 4 strips 5" × WOF.

+ Subcut 2 strips into 8 rectangles 5" × 9½"; each strip yields 4 rectangles.

+ Subcut 2 strips into 12 squares 5" × 5"; each strip yields 8 squares.

Cut 4 strips 3½" × WOF.

Cut 2 strips 2¾" × WOF.

+ Subcut into 8 rectangles 2¾" × 9½"; each strip yields 4 rectangles.

Cut 4 strips 2" × WOF.

Cut 3 strips 1¼" × WOF.

+ Subcut 2 strips into 8 rectangles 1¼" × 5¾"; each strip yields 6 rectangles.

+ Subcut 1 strip into 8 rectangles 1¼" × 5".

BLUE

Cut 4 strips 2" × WOF.

+ Subcut 2 strips into 16 rectangles 2" × 5"; each strip yields 8 rectangles.

ORANGE

Cut 2 squares 5" × 5" and 1 rectangle 5" × 14".

BINDING

Cut 8 strips 2½" × WOF.

finished block	finished quilt	difficulty
13½″ × 13½″	68″ × 68″	✚ ✚

Fabrics: Doe by Carolyn Friedlander for Robert Kaufman Fabrics and Cotton + Steel Basics

instructions

Seam allowances are a scant ¼" unless otherwise noted. Press all seams open unless otherwise noted.

Aqua Plus Units

1. Sew 1 aqua strip and 2 white 3½" × WOF strips together. Repeat to make 2 aqua strip sets.

2. Cut the aqua strip sets into 16 aqua strip units 3½" × 9½".

3. Sew 2 aqua strip units and 1 aqua rectangle together to make an aqua plus unit measuring 9½" × 9½". Repeat to make a total of 8 aqua plus units.

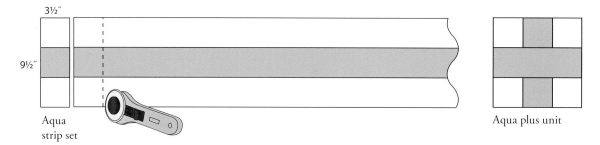

3½"

9½"

Aqua
strip set

Aqua plus unit

Blue Plus Units

1. Sew 1 blue strip and 2 white 2" × WOF strips together. Repeat to make 2 blue strip sets.

2. Cut the blue strip sets into 32 blue strip units 2" × 5".

3. Sew 2 blue strip units and 1 blue rectangle together to make a blue plus unit measuring 5" × 5". Repeat to make a total of 16 blue plus units.

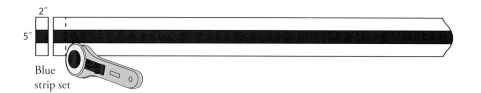

2"

5"

Blue
strip set

Blue plus
unit

Block 1

1. Sew 2 white 5″ squares and 1 orange square together. Repeat to make a total of 2 units.

2. Sew 1 orange rectangle and 2 units from Step 1 together to make Block 1, measuring 14″ × 14″.

Block 1 assembly

TIP *If using directional prints, rotate the plus units within the blocks before assembling the blocks, referring to the quilt top assembly diagram (page 54).*

Block 2

1. Sew 1 aqua plus unit and 2 white 2¾″ × 9½″ rectangles together.

2. Sew the unit from Step 1 and 1 white 5″ × 14″ rectangle together to make Block 2, measuring 14″ × 14″. Repeat to make 4 of Block 2.

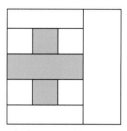

Block 2 assembly

Block 3

1. Sew 1 aqua plus unit and 1 white 5″ × 9½″ rectangle together.

2. Sew 1 blue plus unit and 1 white 5″ × 9½″ rectangle together.

3. Sew the units from Steps 1 and 2 together to make Block 3, measuring 14″ × 14″. Repeat to make 4 of Block 3.

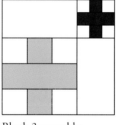

Block 3 assembly

Block 4

1. Sew 1 blue plus unit and 2 white 5″ squares together.

2. Sew together the unit from Step 1, 1 white 3½″ × 14″ rectangle, and 1 white 6½″ × 14″ rectangle to make Block 4, measuring 14″ × 14″. Repeat to make 4 of Block 4.

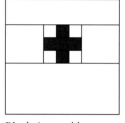

Block 4 assembly

Block 5A

1. Sew 1 blue plus unit and 1 white 1¼″ × 5″ rectangle together.

2. Sew together the unit from Step 1, 1 white 1¼″ × 5¾″ rectangle, and 1 white 5¾″ × 8¾″ rectangle.

3. Sew together the unit from Step 2 and a white 8¾″ × 14″ rectangle to make Block 5A, measuring 14″ × 14″. Repeat to make 4 of Block 5A.

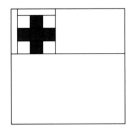

Block 5A assembly

Block 5B

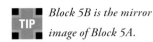 *Block 5B is the mirror image of Block 5A.*

1. Sew 1 blue plus unit and 1 white 1¼″ × 5″ rectangle together.

2. Sew together the unit from Step 1, 1 white 1¼″ × 5¾″ rectangle, and 1 white 5¾ × 8¾″ rectangle.

3. Sew together the unit from Step 2 and a white 8¾″ × 14″ rectangle to make Block 5B, measuring 14″ × 14″. Repeat to make 4 of Block 5B.

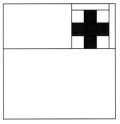

Block 5B assembly

++++++++++++++

Block 6

Each Block 6 is a white 14″ square.

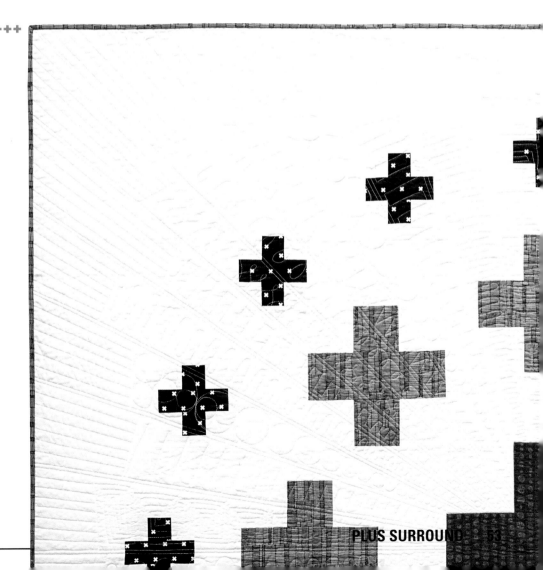

Quilt Top Assembly

1. Arrange and rotate the blocks according to the quilt top block numbers diagram (at right) and quilt top assembly diagram (below).

2. Sew the blocks and fabric pieces into rows. Sew the rows together to make the quilt top, which should measure 68″ × 68″.

6	5A	4	5B	6
5A	3	2	3	5B
4	2	1	2	4
5B	3	2	3	5A
6	5B	4	5A	6

Quilt top block numbers

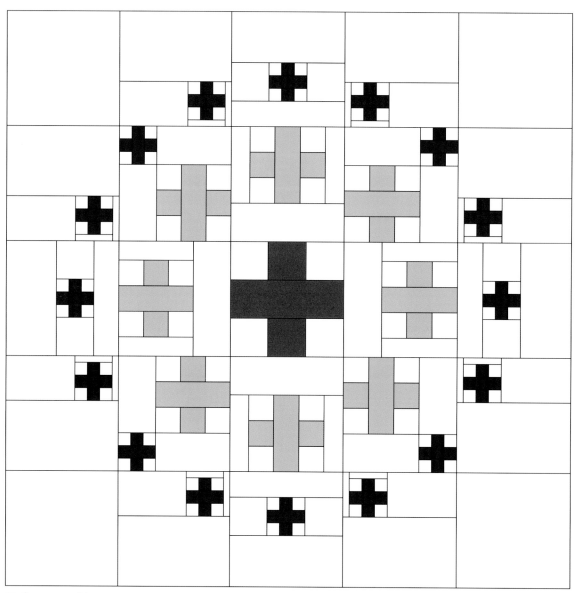

Quilt top assembly

Finishing

Refer to Finishing Your Quilt (page 100) as needed.

1. To make the quilt back, cut the backing fabric into 2 pieces each 76″ × WOF, trim off the selvage edges, and sew the pieces together along the trimmed selvage edges. Trim to approximately 76″ × 76″.

2. Layer the quilt top, batting, and backing. Baste and quilt as desired. Bind and enjoy! This version of *Plus Surround* was quilted in straight lines radiating from the center, with selected fillers enhancing the wedges formed by the straight lines.

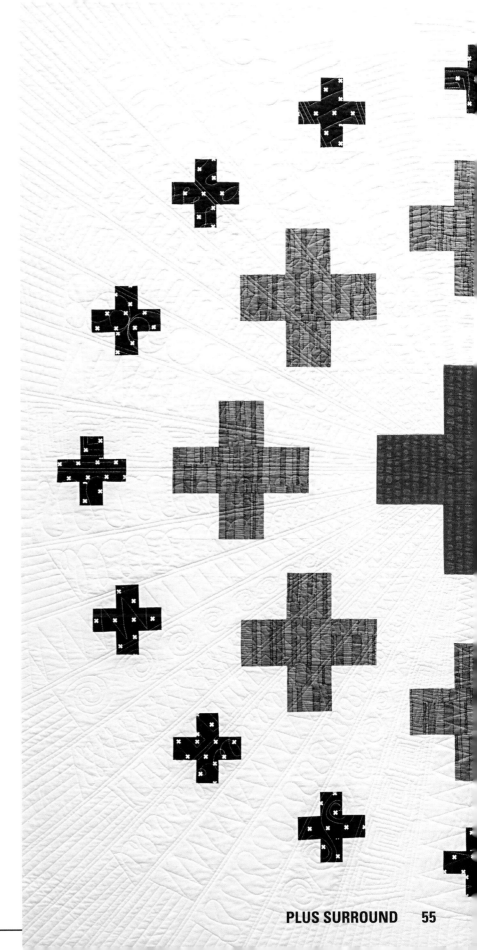

tribal plus

Designed, pieced, and quilted
by Paige Alexander

Plus signs combined with other simple piecing give the effect of more complicated Seminole patchwork in Tribal Plus.

Materials

Yardages are based on fabric that is 40" wide.

Cream: 1¾ yards

Gray: 1½ yards

Yellow: ⅝ yard

Red: ½ yard

Binding: ⅝ yard

Batting: 59" × 71"

Backing: 3¼ yards

Cutting

CREAM

Cut 3 strips 4½" × width of fabric (WOF).

+ Subcut 1 strip into 2 rectangles 4½" × 20".

Cut 16 strips 2½" × WOF.

+ Subcut 7 strips into 42 rectangles 2½" × 6½"; each strip yields 6 rectangles.

+ Subcut 1 strip into 8 rectangles 2½" × 4½".

+ Subcut 1 strip into 4 rectangles 2½" × 4½" and 2 squares 2½" × 2½".

+ Subcut 3 strips into 48 squares 2½" × 2½"; each strip yields 16 squares.

GRAY

Cut 18 strips 2½" × WOF.

+ Subcut 9 strips into 54 rectangles 2½" × 6½"; each strip yields 6 rectangles.

+ Subcut 1 strip into 3 rectangles 2½" × 6½" and 4 squares 2½" × 2½".

+ Subcut 2 strips into 32 squares 2½" × 2½"; each strip yields 16 squares.

YELLOW

Cut 6 strips 2½" × WOF.

+ Subcut 3 strips into 18 rectangles 2½" × 6½"; each strip yields 6 rectangles.

RED

Cut 5 strips 2½" × WOF.

+ Subcut 2 strips into 10 rectangles 2½" × 6½"; each strip yields 6 rectangles.

+ Subcut 1 strip into 4 rectangles 2½" × 4½" and 8 squares 2½" × 2½".

BINDING

Cut 7 strips 2½" × WOF.

*Fabrics: Good Hair Day by Kim Andersson, Petite Fleur by Carolyn Gavin of Ecojot,
and Artisan Cotton by Another Point of View—all for Windham Fabrics*

instructions

Seam allowances are a scant ¼" unless otherwise noted. Press all seams open unless otherwise noted.

Row A

Sew 2 cream 2½" × 4½" rectangles, 6 gray squares, and 5 cream 2½" × 6½" rectangles together to make row A, measuring 2½" × 50½". Repeat to make 6 rows A.

Row A assembly

Row B

Sew 7 cream squares and 6 gray 2½" × 6½" rectangles together to make row B, measuring 2½" × 50½". Repeat to make 6 rows B.

Row B assembly

Row C

1. Sew 2 gray strips and 1 yellow strip together. Repeat to make 3 strip sets. Cut the strip sets into 36 units 2½" × 6½".

2. Sew together 2 units from Step 1 and 1 yellow rectangle to make a yellow Plus block measuring 6½" × 6½". Repeat to make 18 yellow Plus blocks.

Yellow Plus
block assembly

3. Sew 7 gray rectangles and 6 yellow Plus blocks together to make row C, measuring 6½" × 50½". Repeat to make 3 rows C.

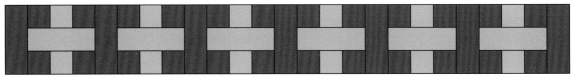

Row C assembly

Row D

1. Sew 2 cream strips and 1 red strip together. Repeat to make 2 strip sets. Cut the strip sets into 20 units 2½″ × 6½″.

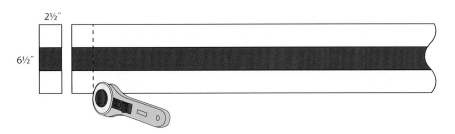

2. Sew together 2 units from Step 1 and 1 red 2½″ × 6½″ rectangle to make a red Plus block measuring 6½″ × 6½″. Repeat to make 10 red Plus blocks.

3. Sew 1 red square and 1 cream square together. Repeat to make 8 units.

4. Sew together 2 units from Step 3 and 1 red 2½″ × 4½″ rectangle to make a partial Plus block measuring 4½″ × 6½″. Repeat to make 4.

5. Sew together 2 partial Plus blocks, 6 cream 2½″ × 6½″ rectangles, and 5 red Plus blocks to make row D, measuring 6½″ × 50½″. Repeat to make 2 rows D.

Red Plus block assembly

Partial Plus block assembly

Quilt Top Assembly

1. Arrange the rows according to the quilt top assembly diagram (next page).

2. Sew the rows together to make the quilt top, which should measure 50½″ × 54½″ before the borders are added.

Borders

1. Sew 1 cream 4½″ × WOF strip and 1 cream 4½″ × 20″ rectangle together end to end. Repeat to make a total of 2 top/bottom strips.

2. Measure the average width of the quilt top, and trim the 2 top/bottom strips to fit (approximately 50½″). Attach the top and bottom borders to the quilt top.

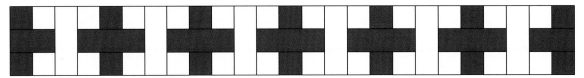

Row D assembly

+++

Finishing

Refer to Finishing Your Quilt (page 100) as needed.

1. To make the quilt back, cut the backing fabric into 2 pieces each 59″ × WOF, trim off the selvage edges, and sew the pieces together along the trimmed selvage edges. Trim to approximately 59″ × 71″.

2. Layer the quilt top, batting, and backing. Baste and quilt as desired. Bind and enjoy! This version of *Tribal Plus* was quilted using echoing chevron designs to highlight the plus signs.

Quilt top assembly

pinwheel plus

Designed and pieced by Cheryl Brickey
and quilted by Johellen George

The plus signs intertwine with pinwheel shapes for a fun lap quilt.

Materials

Yardages are based on fabric that is 40" wide.

White: 3⅛ yards

Pink prints: 6 fat quarters (18" × 20")

Gray: ⅞ yard

Binding: ⅝ yard

Batting: 69" × 66"

Backing: 3⅞ yards

TIP *You can use a larger number of pink fabrics for a scrappier-looking quilt.*

Cutting

WHITE

Cut 7 strips 3⅞" × width of fabric (WOF).

+ Subcut into 72 squares 3⅞" × 3⅞"; each strip yields 11 squares.

Cut 25 strips 3" × WOF.

+ Subcut 1 strip into 2 rectangles 3" × 20".

+ Subcut 3 strips into 12 rectangles 3" × 8"; each strip yields 5 rectangles.

+ Subcut 5 strips into 33 rectangles 3" × 5½"; each strip yields 7 rectangles.

+ Subcut 10 strips into 126 squares 3" × 3"; each strip yields 13 squares.

PINK PRINTS

Cut *each* fat quarter into 3 rectangles 3" × 8" and 6 squares 3" × 3" for a total of 18 rectangles 3" × 8" and 36 squares 3" × 3".

GRAY

Cut 7 strips 3⅞" × WOF.

+ Subcut into 72 squares 3⅞" × 3⅞"; each strip yields 11 squares.

BINDING

Cut 7 strips 2½" × WOF.

finished plus block	finished quilt	difficulty
7½" × 7½"	60½" × 58"	✚ ✚

Fabric: Assorted pink prints and Cotton Couture by Michael Miller Fabrics in Coin and Bright White

instructions

Seam allowances are a scant ¼″ unless otherwise noted. Press all seams open unless otherwise noted.

Plus Blocks

1. Sew 2 white 3″ squares to a pink square. Repeat to make 2 units.

2. Sew 1 pink rectangle and 2 units from Step 1 together to make a Plus block measuring 8″ × 8″. Repeat to make a total of 18 Plus blocks.

Plus block

 Use matching pink fabrics within each Plus block.

Half-Square Triangles

Sew 72 gray and 72 white 3⅞″ squares into 144 half-square triangles measuring 3″ × 3″ using the directions in Making Half-Square Triangles (page 9).

Partial Pinwheel Blocks

 Be sure to double-check the orientation of the half-square triangles before sewing.

1. Sew 1 white 3″ × 5½″ rectangle, 1 half-square triangle, and 1 white 3″ square together to make 1 A unit.

A unit

2. Sew together 3 half-square triangles and 1 white 3″ square to make 1 B unit. Repeat to make 2 B units.

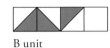

B unit

3. Sew together 1 A unit and 2 B units to make a partial Pinwheel block measuring 8″ × 10½″. Repeat to make 18 partial Pinwheel blocks.

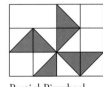

Partial Pinwheel block

 The bottom B unit is rotated 180° relative to the top B unit.

Quilt Top Assembly

1. Sew together 5 white 3″ × 5½″ rectangles, 6 half-square triangles, and 2 white 3″ × 8″ rectangles to make a sashing row measuring 3″ × 55½″. Repeat to make 3 sashing rows.

Sashing row

2. Sew together 1 white 3″ × 8″ rectangle, 3 Plus blocks, and 3 partial Pinwheel blocks to make a block row measuring 8″ × 55½″. Repeat to make 6 block rows.

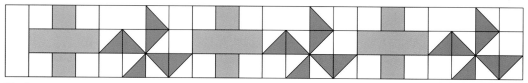

Block row

3. Arrange and rotate the 6 block rows and 3 sashing rows according to the quilt top assembly diagram (next page).

4. Sew the block rows and sashing rows together to make the quilt top, which should measure 55½″ × 52½″ before the borders are added.

+++

Borders

1. Sew 1 white 3″ × WOF strip and 1 white 3″ × 20″ rectangle together end to end. Repeat to make a total of 2 pieced side strips.

2. Measure the average height of the quilt top, and trim the 2 pieced side strips to fit (approximately 52½″). Attach the side borders to the quilt top.

3. Sew 2 white 3″ × WOF strips together end to end. Repeat to make a total of 2 pieced top/bottom strips.

4. Measure the average width of the quilt top, and trim the 2 top/bottom strips to fit (approximately 60½″). Attach the top and bottom borders to the quilt top.

Finishing

Refer to Finishing Your Quilt (page 100) as needed.

1. To make the quilt back, cut the backing fabric into 2 pieces each 69″ × WOF, trim off the selvage edges, and sew the pieces together along the trimmed selvage edges. Trim to approximately 69″ × 66″.

2. Layer the quilt top, batting, and backing. Baste and quilt as desired. Bind and enjoy! This version of *Pinwheel Plus* was quilted in a double looping pattern.

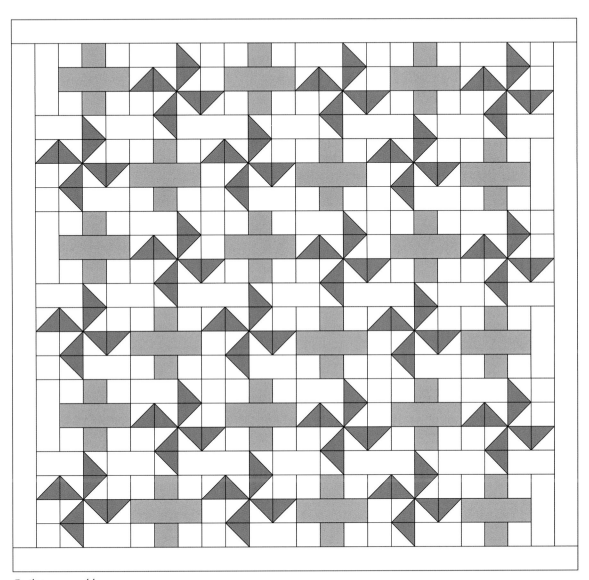

Quilt top assembly

kaleidoscope plus

Designed, pieced, and quilted
by Cheryl Brickey

*This interlocking ring design is formed using traditional Kaleidoscope
blocks in combination with plus signs. Kaleidoscope Plus is made using
a combination of paper-pieced blocks and traditionally pieced blocks.*

Materials

*Yardages are based on
fabric that is 40" wide.*

Dark gray: 1⅝ yards

Light gray: 3¾ yards

White: 1¼ yards

Dark blue: ⅝ yard

Blue print: ⅝ yard

Binding: ⅝ yard

Batting: 72" × 72"

Backing: 4 yards

Foundation paper:
34 sheets 8½" × 11"

Cutting

DARK GRAY

**Cut 11 strips 4¾" × width
of fabric (WOF).**

+ Subcut into 64 rectangles
  4¾" × 6"; each strip
  yields 6 rectangles.

LIGHT GRAY

Cut 1 strip 6½" × WOF.

+ Subcut into 4 squares
  6½" × 6½".

Cut 7 strips 6" × WOF.

+ Subcut 6 strips into
  52 rectangles 6" × 4";
  each strip yields 10 rectangles.

+ Subcut 1 strip into
  16 rectangles 6" × 2½".

Cut 9 strips 5" × WOF.

+ Subcut 1 strip into
  2 rectangles 5" × 20".

+ Subcut 1 strip into
  6 rectangles 5" × 6½".

+ Subcut 1 strip into
  2 rectangles 5" × 6½" and
  4 squares 5" × 5".

Cut 4 strips 4" × WOF.

+ Subcut into 32 squares
  4" × 4"; each strip yields
  10 squares.

Cut 3 strips 3½" × WOF.

+ Subcut 1 strip into
  4 rectangles 3½" × 5".

+ Subcut 1 strip into
  16 rectangles 3½" × 2".

+ Subcut 1 strip into
  24 rectangles 3½" × 1½".

Cut 3 strips 1½" × WOF.

WHITE

Cut 6 strips 5¾" × WOF.

+ Subcut into 64 rectangles
  5¾" × 3¼"; each strip
  yields 12 rectangles.

DARK BLUE

Cut 4 strips 4" × WOF.

+ Subcut into 32 squares
  4" × 4"; each strip yields
  10 squares.

BLUE PRINT

Cut 3 strips 3½" × WOF.

+ Subcut into 12 rectangles
  3½" × 7½"; each strip
  yields 5 rectangles.

Cut 3 strips 2½" × WOF.

BINDING

Cut 7 strips 2½" × WOF.

finished block	finished quilt	difficulty
9″ × 9″	63½″ × 63½″	✚ ✚ ✚

Fabric: Blueberry Park by Karen Lewis Textiles for Robert Kaufman Fabrics

instructions

Seam allowances are a scant ¼″ unless otherwise noted. Press all seams open unless otherwise noted. Use the foundation paper-piecing directions (page 12) to sew the paper-pieced blocks.

Kaleidoscope Blocks

1. Trace or photocopy the *Kaleidoscope Plus* foundation patterns A, B, and C onto foundation paper the number of times indicated.

2. Paper piece each foundation using the following precut pieces.

Kaleidoscope Plus Foundation A

Use Foundation A (page 107); make 22.

Segment A1	Dark gray rectangle 4¾″ × 6″
Segment A2	White rectangle 5¾″ × 3¼″
Segment A3	Light gray rectangle 6″ × 4″
Segment A4	Dark gray rectangle 4¾″ × 6″
Segment A5	Light gray rectangle 6″ × 4″
Segment A6	White rectangle 5¾″ × 3¼″

Kaleidoscope Plus Foundation B

Use Foundation B (page 108); make 4.

Segment B1	Dark gray rectangle 4¾″ × 6″
Segment B2	White rectangle 5¾″ × 3¼″
Segment B3	Light gray square 6½″ × 6½″

Kaleidoscope Plus Foundation C

Use Foundation C (page 109); make 8.

Segment C1	Dark gray rectangle 4¾″ × 6″
Segment C2	White rectangle 5¾″ × 3¼″
Segment C3	Light gray rectangle 6″ × 4″
Segment C4	Dark gray rectangle 4¾″ × 6″
Segment C5	Light gray rectangle 6″ × 2½″
Segment C6	White rectangle 5¾″ × 3¼″
Segment C7	Light gray rectangle 6″ × 2½″

3. Trim each unit along the foundation's outer seamlines.

4. Sew 2 foundations A together to make a full Kaleidoscope block measuring 9½″ × 9½″. Repeat to make 9 full Kaleidoscope blocks.

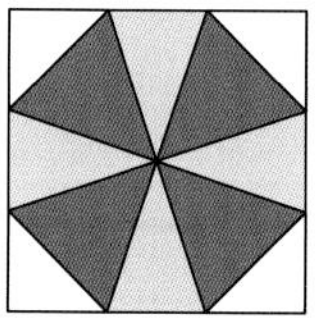

Full Kaleidoscope block

5. Sew foundations A and B together to make a three-quarter Kaleidoscope block measuring 9½″ × 9½″. Repeat to make 4 three-quarter Kaleidoscope blocks.

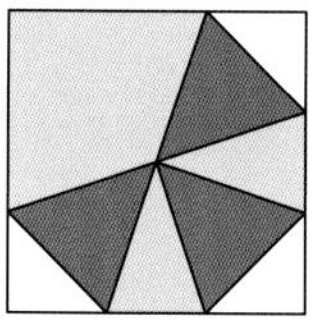

Three-quarter Kaleidoscope block

6. The 8 foundations C are the half-Kaleidoscope blocks measuring 5″ × 9½″.

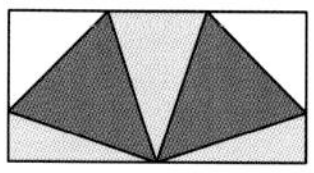

Half-Kaleidoscope block

Plus Blocks

1. Sew 32 dark blue and 32 light gray 4″ squares into 64 half-square triangles measuring 3½″ × 3½″ using the directions in Making Half-Square Triangles (page 9). Set 16 aside for use in the Outer blocks.

2. Sew 1 blue print strip and 1 light gray 1½″ × WOF strip together. Repeat to make 3 strip sets. Cut the strip sets into 24 units 3½″ × 3½″.

3. Sew 1 blue print rectangle and 2 light gray 1½″ × 3½″ rectangles together to make a unit measuring 3½″ × 9½″. Repeat to make 12 units.

4. Sew 2 half-square triangles and 1 unit from Step 2 together to make a unit measuring 3½″ × 9½″. Repeat to make 24 units.

5. Sew 1 unit from Step 3 and 2 units from Step 4 together to make a Plus block measuring 9½″ × 9½″. Repeat to make 12 Plus blocks.

Plus block

Outer Blocks

1. Sew 1 half-square triangle, 1 light gray 2″ × 3½″ rectangle, and 1 light gray 5″ × 6½″ rectangle together to make a first Outer block measuring 5″ × 9½″. Repeat to make 4 first Outer blocks.

First Outer block

2. Sew 1 half-square triangle, 1 light gray 2″ × 3½″ rectangle, and 1 light gray 5″ × 6½″ rectangle together to make a second Outer block measuring 5″ × 9½″. Repeat to make 4 second Outer blocks.

Second Outer block

TIP *Note that the first and second outer blocks are mirror images of each other. Be sure to double-check placement and the orientation of the half-square triangles within each block.*

3. Sew 2 half-square triangles, 2 light gray 2″ × 3½″ rectangles, and 1 light gray 3½″ × 5″ rectangle together to make a third Outer block measuring 5″ × 9½″. Repeat to make 4 third Outer blocks.

Third Outer block

Quilt Top Assembly

1. Arrange and rotate the following according to the quilt top assembly diagram (next page).

+ 9 full Kaleidoscope blocks

+ 4 three-quarter Kaleidoscope blocks

+ 8 half-Kaleidoscope blocks

+ 12 Plus blocks

+ 4 first Outer blocks

+ 4 second Outer blocks

+ 4 third Outer blocks

+ 4 light gray 5″ squares

2. Sew the blocks into rows. Sew the rows together to make the quilt top, which should measure 54½″ × 54½″ before the borders are added.

Borders

1. Sew 1 light gray 5″ × WOF strip and 1 light gray 5″ × 20″ rectangle together end to end. Repeat to make a total of 2 pieced side strips.

2. Measure the average height of the quilt top, and trim the 2 pieced side strips to fit (approximately 54½″). Attach the side borders to the quilt top.

3. Sew 2 light gray 5″ × WOF strips together end to end. Repeat to make a total of 2 pieced top/bottom strips.

4. Measure the average width of the quilt top, and trim the 2 top/bottom strips to fit (approximately 63½″). Attach the top and bottom borders to the quilt top.

Finishing

Refer to Finishing Your Quilt (page 100) as needed.

1. To make the quilt back, cut the backing fabric into 2 pieces each 72 × WOF, trim off the selvage edges, and sew the pieces together along the trimmed selvage edges. Trim to approximately 72″ × 72″.

2. Layer the quilt top, batting, and backing. Baste and quilt as desired. Bind and enjoy! This version of *Kaleidoscope Plus* was quilted in a meandering pattern.

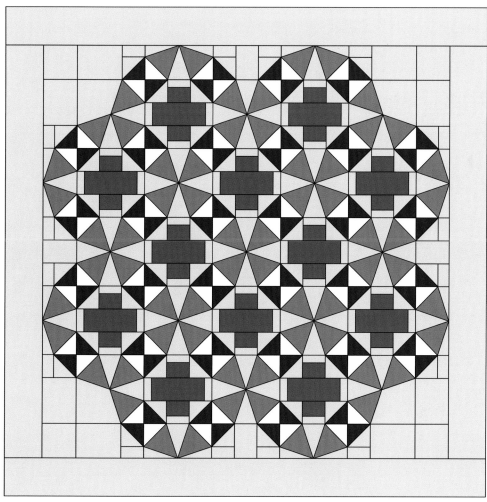

Quilt top assembly

bear claw plus

Designed by Cheryl Brickey, pieced by Paige Alexander, and quilted by Johellen George

The addition of a plus sign and alternating block color schemes into a traditional Bear Claw pattern creates an interesting secondary star design.

Materials

Yardages are based on fabric that is 40" wide.

White: 2½ yards

Pink: 2⅝ yards

Binding: ⅝ yard

Batting: 72" × 72"

Backing: 4 yards

Cutting

WHITE

Cut 3 strips 6½" × width of fabric (WOF).

+ Subcut into 16 squares 6½" × 6½"; each strip yields 6 squares.

Cut 8 strips 4" × WOF.

+ Subcut into 72 squares 4" × 4"; each strip yields 10 squares.

Cut 7 strips 3½" × WOF.

+ Subcut 1 strip into 4 rectangles 3½" × 9½".

+ Subcut 2 strips into 12 rectangles 3½" × 6½"; each strip yields 6 rectangles.

+ Subcut 1 strip into 1 rectangle 3½" × 9½" and 4 rectangles 3½" × 6½".

+ Subcut 3 strips into 26 squares 3½" × 3½"; each strip yields 11 squares.

PINK

Cut 4 strips 6½" × WOF.

+ Subcut into 20 squares 6½" × 6½"; each strip yields 6 squares.

Cut 8 strips 4" × WOF.

+ Subcut into 72 squares 4" × 4"; each strip yields 10 squares.

Cut 8 strips 3½" × WOF.

+ Subcut 1 strip into 4 rectangles 3½" × 9½".

+ Subcut 4 strips into 20 rectangles 3½" × 6½"; each strip yields 6 rectangles.

+ Subcut 3 strips into 28 squares 3½" × 3½"; each strip yields 11 squares.

BINDING

Cut 7 strips 2½" × WOF.

Fabrics: Rhoda Ruth by Elizabeth Hartman and Kona Cotton solids in White—both for Robert Kaufman Fabrics

instructions

Seam allowances are a scant ¼″ unless otherwise noted. Press all seams open unless otherwise noted.

Half-Square Triangles

Sew 72 white and 72 pink 4″ squares into 144 half-square triangles measuring 3½″ × 3½″ using the directions in Making Half-Square Triangles (page 9).

Pink Bear Claw Blocks

 TIP *Double-check the orientation of the half-square triangles before sewing the blocks together.*

1. Sew together 2 half-square triangles and 1 pink 3½″ square.

2. Sew together 2 half-square triangles and 1 pink 6½″ square.

3. Sew the units from Steps 1 and 2 together to make a pink claw unit measuring 9½″ × 9½″. Repeat to make a total of 20 pink claw units.

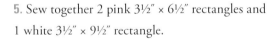

Pink claw unit

4. Sew together 1 pink 3½″ × 6½″ rectangle, 1 white 3½″ square, and 2 pink claw units. Make 2.

5. Sew together 2 pink 3½″ × 6½″ rectangles and 1 white 3½″ × 9½″ rectangle.

6. Sew together 2 units from Step 4 and 1 unit from Step 5 to make a pink Bear Claw block measuring 21½″ × 21½″. Repeat Steps 4–6 to make a total of 5 pink Bear Claw blocks.

Pink Bear Claw block

White Bear Claw Blocks

1. Sew together 2 half-square triangles and 1 white 3½″ square.

2. Sew together 2 half-square triangles and 1 white 6½″ square.

3. Sew the units from Steps 1 and 2 together to make a white claw unit measuring 9½″ × 9½″. Repeat to make a total of 16 white claw units.

White claw unit

4. Sew together 1 white 3½″ × 6½″ rectangle, 1 pink 3½″ square, and 2 white claw units. Make 2.

5. Sew together 2 white 3½″ × 6½″ rectangles and 1 pink 3½″ × 9½″ rectangle.

6. Sew together 2 units from Step 4 and 1 unit from Step 5 to make a white Bear Claw block measuring 21½″ × 21½″. Repeat Steps 4–6 to make a total of 4 white Bear Claw blocks.

White Bear Claw block

Quilt Top Assembly

1. Arrange the 5 pink and 4 white Bear Claw blocks according to the quilt top assembly diagram.

2. Sew the blocks into rows. Sew the rows together to make the quilt top, which should measure 63½" × 63½".

Quilt top assembly

Finishing

Refer to Finishing Your Quilt (page 100) as needed.

1. To make the quilt back, cut the backing fabric into 2 pieces each 72″ × WOF, trim off the selvage edges, and sew the pieces together along the trimmed selvage edges. Trim to approximately 72″ × 72″.

2. Layer the quilt top, batting, and backing. Baste and quilt as desired. Bind and enjoy! This version of *Bear Claw Plus* was quilted with swirls, pebbles, and straight lines to highlight the plus signs within the bear paws.

intertwined

Designed by Cheryl Brickey and pieced and
quilted by Paige Alexander

*The nested plus signs combine with a border to create a design of pluses
floating on a background. A design wall (or floor) is helpful to lay out
the fabric pieces for* Intertwined, *as it does not contain repeating blocks.*

Materials

*Yardages are based on
fabric that is 40″ wide.*

Prints: 12 fat quarters
(18″ × 20″)

White: 3⅛ yards

Binding: ¾ yard

Batting: 77″ × 97″

Backing: 5½ yards

Cutting

PRINTS

Cut *each* print fat quarter into
3 rectangles 4½″ × 12½″ and
6 squares 4½″ × 4½″ according
to the cutting diagram.

WHITE

Cut 8 strips 8½″ × width of fabric (WOF).

Cut 7 strips 4½″ × WOF.

+ Subcut 2 strips into 4 rectangles
4½″ × 16½″; each strip yields 2 rectangles.

+ Subcut 2 strips into 6 rectangles 4½″ × 8½″
and 6 squares 4½″ × 4½″; each strip yields
3 rectangles and 3 squares.

+ Subcut 3 strips into 20 squares 4½″ × 4½″;
each strip yields 8 squares.

BINDING

Cut 9 strips 2½″ × WOF.

Cutting diagram:

20″

4½″ × 12½″	4½″ × 12½″	4½″ × 12½″	4½″ × 4½″
			4½″ × 4½″
			4½″ × 4½″
4½″ × 4½″	4½″ × 4½″	4½″ × 4½″	Scrap

18″

Cutting

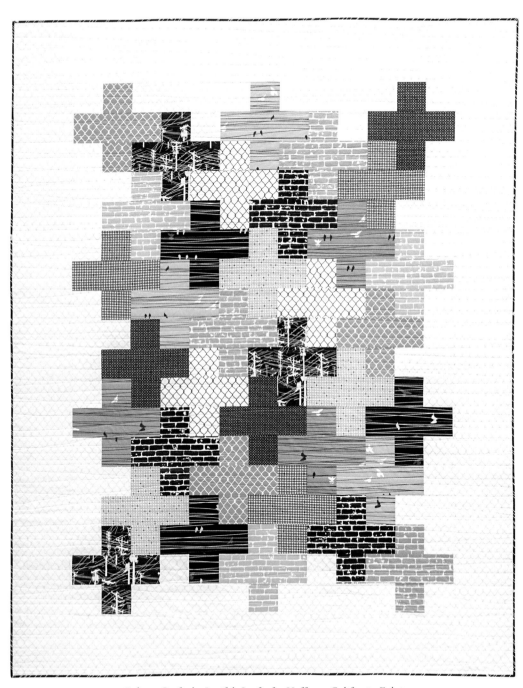

Fabric: Grafic by Latifah Saafir for Hoffman California Fabrics

instructions

Seam allowances are a scant ¼″ unless otherwise noted. Press all seams open unless otherwise noted.

Quilt Top Assembly

1. On a design wall (or floor), lay out the fabric pieces in a pleasing arrangement, following the quilt top assembly diagram (at right).

2. Sew the pieces into rows. Sew the rows together to make the quilt top, which should measure 52½″ × 72½″ before the borders are added.

Borders

1. Sew 2 white 8½″ × WOF strips together end to end. Repeat to make a total of 2 pieced side strips.

2. Measure the average height of the quilt top, and trim the 2 side strips to fit (approximately 72½″). Attach the side borders to the quilt top.

3. Sew 2 white 8½″ × WOF strips together end to end. Repeat to make a total of 2 pieced top/bottom strips.

4. Measure the average width of the quilt top, and trim the 2 top/bottom strips to fit (approximately 68½″). Attach the top and bottom borders to the quilt top.

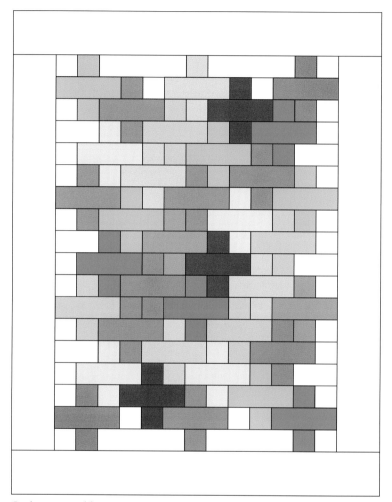

Quilt top assembly

Finishing

Refer to Finishing Your Quilt (page 100) as needed.

1. To make the quilt back, cut the backing fabric into 2 pieces each 99″ × WOF, trim off the selvage edges, and sew the pieces together along the trimmed selvage edges. Trim to approximately 77″ × 97″.

2. Layer the quilt top, batting, and backing. Baste and quilt as desired. Bind and enjoy! This version of *Intertwined* was quilted with an organic horizontal line pattern.

petal plus

Designed by Cheryl Brickey, appliquéd and pieced by
Paige Alexander, and quilted by Johellen George

Petal Plus *combines appliquéd petals with plus signs for a fresh
and modern bed quilt design.*

Materials

*Yardages are based on
fabric that is 40" wide.*

Aqua: 1⅝ yards

White: 5½ yards

Red: ⅝ yard

Binding: ¾ yard

Batting: 76" × 96"

Backing: 5⅓ yards

**Paper-backed fusible
web:** 20 rectangles
5" × 20"

**Iron-on tear-away
stabilizer:** 24 squares
9½" × 9½"

Cutting

AQUA

**Cut 10 strips 5" × width of fabric
(WOF).**

+ Subcut into 20 rectangles 5" × 20".

WHITE

Cut 8 strips 11½" × WOF.

+ Subcut into 24 squares 11½" × 11½";
  each strip yields 3 squares.

Cut 4 strips 9½" × WOF.

Cut 1 strip 8½" × WOF.

Cut 4 strips 6½" × WOF.

Cut 1 strip 6" × WOF.

Cut 5 strips 3" × WOF.

+ Subcut 3 strips into 10 rectangles
  3" × 8½"; each strip yields 4 rectangles.

+ Subcut 2 strips into 10 rectangles
  3" × 6"; each strip yields 6 rectangles.

RED

Cut 6 strips 3" × WOF.

+ Subcut 3 strips into 15 rectangles
  3" × 8"; each strip yields 5 rectangles.

BINDING

Cut 9 strips 2½" × WOF.

Fabrics: Farm Fun by Stacy Iest Hsu and Bella Solids for Moda Fabrics

instructions

Seam allowances are a scant ¼″ unless otherwise noted. Press all seams open unless otherwise noted.

Petal Blocks

See Fusible Machine Appliqué (page 9) to appliqué the blocks.

1. Create 96 appliqué shapes using the *Petal Plus* petal pattern (page 110), aqua rectangles, and paper-backed fusible web. Arranging the petal appliqué shapes at a 45° angle on the rectangles allows for more efficient use of the fabric.

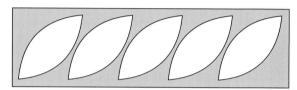

Petal appliqué shape layout

+-

TIP *The petal appliqué shapes can also be cut with any of the AccuQuilt fabric cutting systems using the GO! Orange Peel 4½″ (#55455) fabric cutting die to save time.*

+-

2. Fold a white 11½″ square in half horizontally, press to make a crease, and repeat vertically to aid in petal placement (shown as dotted lines on the petal placement guide).

3. Center, arrange, and fuse 4 appliqué petal shapes into a circle 1¼″ from each side of the square.

4. Center and iron stabilizer onto the back of the square. Repeat to make 24 Petal blocks.

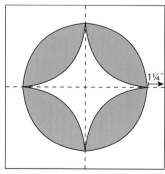

Petal placement

5. Using a zigzag satin stitch, appliqué around the inner sides of the petal shapes, pivoting where the petals touch. Without stopping, pivot and appliqué completely around the circle formed by the petals according to the petal stitch path diagram. Carefully remove the stabilizer.

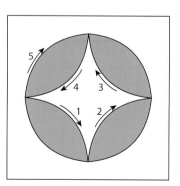

Petal stitch path

6. Trim the Petal blocks to 11″ × 11″.

Sashing

1. Sew 1 red strip and 1 white 8½" × WOF strip together. Cut the strip set into 6 single sashing pieces 3" × 11".

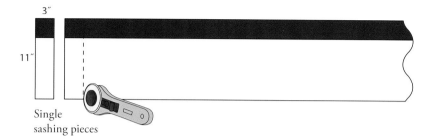

Single
sashing pieces

2. Sew 2 red strips and 1 white 6" × WOF strip together. Cut the strip set into 12 double sashing pieces 3" × 11".

Double
sashing pieces

3. Sew together 2 white 3" × 8½" rectangles, 3 red rectangles, and 2 white 3" × 6" rectangles to make a sashing row measuring 3" × 50". Repeat to make 5 sashing rows.

Sashing row

Quilt Top Assembly

1. Arrange the Petal blocks in a 4 × 6 arrangement along with the single sashing pieces, double sashing pieces, and the sashing rows according to the quilt top assembly diagram (next page).

2. Sew the Petal blocks, single sashing pieces, and double sashing pieces into rows. Sew the rows and the sashing rows together to make the quilt top, which should measure 50" × 76" before the borders are added.

Borders

1. Sew 2 white 9½" × WOF strips together end to end. Repeat to make a total of 2 pieced side strips.

2. Measure the average height of the quilt top, and trim the 2 pieced side strips to fit (approximately 76"). Attach the side borders to the quilt top.

3. Sew 2 white 6½" × WOF strips together end to end. Repeat to make a total of 2 pieced top/bottom strips.

4. Measure the average width of the quilt top, and trim the 2 top/bottom strips to fit (approximately 68"). Attach the top and bottom borders to the quilt top.

Finishing

Refer to Finishing Your Quilt (page 100) as needed.

1. To make the quilt back, cut the backing fabric into 2 pieces each 96" × WOF, trim off the selvage edges, and sew the pieces together along the trimmed selvage edges. Trim to approximately 76" × 96".

2. Layer the quilt top, batting, and backing. Baste and quilt as desired. Bind and enjoy! This version of *Petal Plus* was quilted in an allover leaf and feather combination.

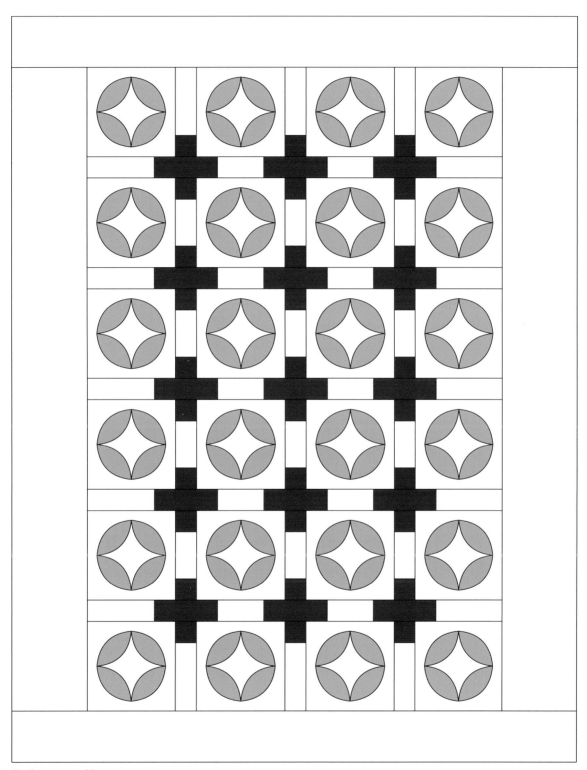

Quilt top assembly

transparency chains

Designed, pieced, and quilted
by Cheryl Brickey

Transparency Chains combines a plus sign design with aspects of transparency in an Irish Chain setting. Strip piecing makes the block construction quick and easy.

Materials

Yardages are based on fabric that is 40" wide.

Gray: 1⅛ yards

White: 4¾ yards

Light blue: ⅜ yard

Medium blue: ⅜ yard

Dark blue: ⅝ yard

Yellow: ¼ yard

Binding: ¾ yard

Batting: 79" × 99"

Backing: 5½ yards

Cutting

GRAY

Cut 14 strips 2½" × width of fabric (WOF).

WHITE

Cut 7 strips 6½" × WOF.

+ Subcut 3 strips into 9 rectangles 6½" × 10½"; each strip yields 3 rectangles.

+ Subcut 1 strip into 1 rectangle 6½" × 10½" and 4 squares 6½" × 6½".

Cut 13 strips 4½" × WOF.

+ Subcut 1 strip into 2 rectangles 4½" × 20".

Cut 8 strips 4" × WOF.

+ Subcut into 72 squares 4" × 4"; each strip yields 10 squares.

Cut 9 strips 2½" × WOF.

LIGHT BLUE

Cut 7 strips 1½" × WOF.

MEDIUM BLUE

Cut 7 strips 1½" × WOF.

DARK BLUE

Cut 7 strips 2" × WOF.

Cut 4 strips 1½" × WOF.

YELLOW

Cut 4 strips 1½" × WOF.

+ Subcut 2 strips into 18 rectangles 1½" × 3½"; each strip yields 11 rectangles.

BINDING

Cut 9 strips 2½" × WOF.

finished block	finished quilt	difficulty
10″ × 10″	70½″ × 90½″	✚ ✚

Fabric: Cirrus Solids by Cloud9 Fabrics in Amazon, Limestone, Rain, Shadow, Sprout, and Turquoise

instructions

Seam allowances are a scant ¼″ unless otherwise noted. Press all seams open unless otherwise noted.

Chain Blocks

1. Sew 2 gray strips and 1 white 6½″ × WOF strip together. Repeat to make 3 strip sets. Cut the strip sets into 48 A units 2½″ × 10½″.

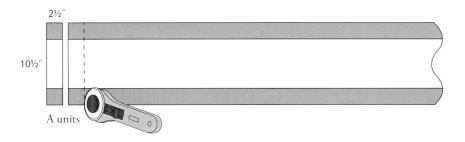

2½″

10½″

A units

2. Sew 2 gray strips and 3 white 2½″ × WOF strips together. Repeat to make 3 strip sets. Cut the strip sets into 48 B units 2½″ × 10½″.

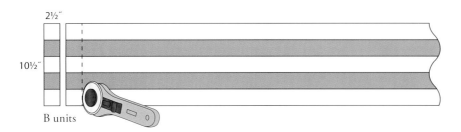

2½″

10½″

B units

3. Sew 1 gray strip and 2 white 4½″ × WOF strips together. Repeat to make 2 strip sets. Cut the strip sets into 31 C units 2½″ × 10½″.

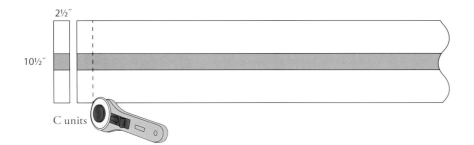

2½″

10½″

C units

4. Sew together 2 A units, 2 B units, and 1 C unit to make a full Chain block measuring 10½″ × 10½″. Repeat to make a total of 17 full Chain blocks.

Full Chain block

5. Sew together 1 A unit, 1 B unit, and 1 C unit to make a partial Chain block measuring 6½″ × 10½″. Repeat to make a total of 14 partial Chain blocks.

Partial Chain block

Transparency Plus Blocks

1. Sew 1 light blue strip, 1 medium blue strip, and 1 dark blue 2″ × WOF strip together. Repeat to make 7 strip sets. Cut the strip sets into 72 D units 3½″ × 4″.

3½″

4″

D units

2. Sew 2 dark blue 1½″ × WOF strips and 1 yellow strip together. Repeat to make 2 strip sets. Cut the strip sets into 36 E units 1½″ × 3½″.

1½″

3½″

E units

3. Sew 2 E units and 1 yellow 1½″ × 3½″ rectangle together to make a plus unit measuring 3½″ × 3½″. Repeat to make a total of 18 plus units.

Plus unit

4. Sew together 1 plus unit, 4 D units, and 4 white 4″ squares to make a Transparency Plus block measuring 10½″ × 10½″. Repeat to make a total of 18 Transparency Plus blocks.

Transparency
Plus block

Quilt Top Assembly

1. Arrange and rotate the following blocks and fabric pieces according to the quilt top assembly diagram (next page).

+ 17 full Chain blocks

+ 14 partial Chain blocks

+ 18 Transparency Plus blocks

+ 10 white 6½″ × 10½″ rectangles

+ 4 white 6½″ squares

2. Sew the blocks and fabric pieces into rows. Sew the rows together to make the quilt top, which should measure 62½″ × 82½″ before the borders are added.

Borders

1. Sew 2 white 4½″ × WOF strips and 1 white 4½″ × 20″ rectangle together end to end. Repeat to make a total of 2 pieced side strips.

2. Measure the average height of the quilt top, and trim the 2 pieced side strips to fit (approximately 82½″). Attach the side borders to the quilt top.

3. Sew 2 white 4½″ × WOF strips together end to end. Repeat to make a total of 2 pieced top/bottom strips.

4. Measure the average width of the quilt top, and trim the 2 pieced top/bottom strips to fit (approximately 70½″). Attach the top and bottom borders to the quilt top.

Finishing

Refer to Finishing Your Quilt (page 100) as needed.

1. To make the quilt back, cut the backing fabric into 2 pieces each 99″ × WOF, trim off the selvage edges, and sew the pieces together along the trimmed selvage edges. Trim to approximately 79″ × 99″.

2. Layer the quilt top, batting, and backing. Baste and quilt as desired. Bind and enjoy! This version of *Transparency Chains* was quilted in an allover paisley pattern.

Quilt top assembly

celestial

Designed and pieced by Cheryl Brickey
and quilted by Johellen George

Celestial *uses large 24" blocks to create a quick and easy queen-size
quilt. The plus signs appear to shine in the night sky.*

Materials

*Yardages are based on
fabric that is 40" wide.*

Prints: 16 fat eighths
(10" × 18")

Blue: 7¼ yards

Binding: ⅞ yard

Batting: 105" × 105"

Backing: 8¾ yards

Cutting

PRINTS

**Cut the following pieces from *each* fat
eighth according to the cutting diagram:**

+ 1 (E) rectangle 12½" × 4½"

+ 1 (K) rectangle 6½" × 2½"

+ 2 (C) squares 4½" × 4½"

+ 2 (J) squares 2½" × 2½"

BLUE

Cut 8 strips 10½" × width of fabric (WOF).

+ Subcut into 16 (M) rectangles
  10½" × 16½" and 16 (O) rectangles
  10½" × 2½"; each strip yields
  2 M rectangles and 2 O rectangles.

Cut 13 strips 6½" × WOF.

+ Subcut 8 strips into 16 (D) rectangles
  6½" × 14½" and 32 (N) rectangles
  6½" × 2½"; each strip yields
  2 D rectangles and 4 N rectangles.

+ Subcut 3 strips into 16 (A) squares
  6½" × 6½"; each strip yields 6 squares.

+ Subcut 2 strips into 16 (G) rectangles
  6½" × 4½"; each strip yields 8 rectangles.

Cut 14 strips 4½" × WOF.

+ Subcut 8 strips into 16 (H) rectangles
  4½" × 14½" and 32 (B) rectangles
  4½" × 2½"; each strip yields
  2 H rectangles and 4 B rectangles.

+ Subcut 6 strips into 16 (F) rectangles
  4½" × 10½"; each strip yields
  3 rectangles.

Cut 4 strips 2½" × WOF.

+ Subcut into 64 (L) squares 2½" × 2½";
  each strip yields 16 squares.

BINDING

Cut 10 strips 2½" × WOF.

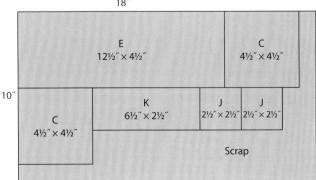

Cutting

finished block	finished quilt	difficulty
24″ × 24″	96½″ × 96½″	✚

Fabrics: Cotton + Steel prints and Cotton Supreme Solids by RJR Studio for RJR Fabrics in Indigo

instructions

Seam allowances are a scant ¼" unless otherwise noted. Press all seams open unless otherwise noted.

Block Assembly

 **TIP** *Use matching fabrics for pieces C and E in the large plus signs and matching fabrics for pieces J and K in the small plus signs.*

1. Sew pieces A, B, C, and D together to make row 1, measuring 6½" × 24½".

Row 1

2. Sew pieces B, E, and F together to make row 2, measuring 4½" × 24½".

Row 2

3. Sew pieces G, C, and H together to make row 3, measuring 4½" × 24½".

Row 3

4. Sew together 2 L pieces and a J piece. Repeat to make 2 units. Sew the 2 units and 1 K piece together to make a small plus unit measuring 6½" × 6½".

Small plus unit

5. Sew an M piece, an O piece, 2 N pieces, and a small plus unit together to make row 4, measuring 10½" × 24½".

Row 4

6. Sew rows 1, 2, 3, and 4 together to make a Double Plus block measuring 24½" × 24½". Repeat Steps 1–6 to make 16 blocks.

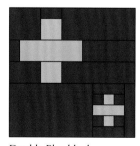
Double Plus block

Quilt Top Assembly

1. Arrange the blocks in a 4 × 4 layout, rotating the Double Plus blocks to give a random appearance to the plus signs according to the quilt top assembly diagram.

2. Sew the blocks into rows. Sew the rows together to make the quilt top, which should measure 96½" × 96½".

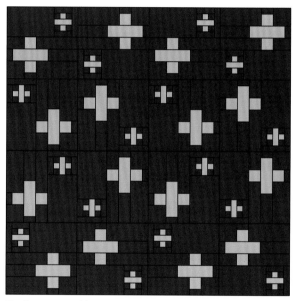
Quilt top assembly

Finishing

Refer to Finishing Your Quilt (page 100) as needed.

1. To make the quilt back, cut the backing fabric into 3 pieces each 105" × WOF, trim off the selvage edges, and sew the pieces together along the trimmed selvage edges. Trim to approximately 105" × 105".

2. Layer the quilt top, batting, and backing. Baste and quilt as desired. Bind and enjoy! This version of *Celestial* was quilted in a large meandering rectangular pattern.

finishing your quilt

borders

Side borders are generally sewn on first. When you have finished the quilt top, measure the average height. This will be the length to cut the side borders. Place pins at the centers of all four sides of the quilt top, as well as in the center of each side border strip. Pin the side borders to the quilt top first, matching the center pins. Using a ¼″ seam allowance, sew the borders to the quilt top, and press the seams open or toward the border.

Measure the average width of the quilt top including the side borders. This will be the length to cut the top and bottom borders. Repeat pinning, sewing, and pressing.

backing

Throughout the book, yardages are given to make the backing a minimum of 8″ longer and wider than the quilt top so that the backing extends 4″ past the quilt top on all sides. Trim away the selvages from the backing fabric, and piece using ½″ seam allowances. Cut to the desired size.

To economize, you may instead piece the back from any leftover quilting fabrics or blocks in your collection.

TIP *For larger quilts, we like using 108″-wide backing fabric rather than piecing sections of 40″ fabric to save valuable time and often yardage.*

batting

Cut the batting approximately 8″ longer and wider than your quilt top. In projects throughout this book, we used 100% cotton Warm & White batting by The Warm Company, which can be quilted leaving up to 10″ open between quilting lines. Note that your batting choice will affect how much quilting is necessary for the quilt. Check the manufacturer's instructions to see how far apart the quilting lines can be.

layering

Spread the backing wrong side up, and tape the edges down with masking tape. (If you are working on carpet, you can use T-pins to secure the backing to the carpet.) Center the batting on top, smoothing out any folds. Place the quilt top right side up on top of the batting and backing, making sure it is centered.

basting

Basting keeps the quilt sandwich layers from shifting while you are quilting.

Our favorite basting method is using a temporary spray adhesive. We prefer 505 Spray and Fix temporary fabric adhesive by ODIF USA. It saves valuable time, and you can start quilting right away. Starting with the backing and batting, work in sections and apply the spray baste between the layers. Repeat with the batting and quilt top. Be sure to follow the manufacturer's directions, use the spray in a well-ventilated area, and protect the surroundings from overspray.

Another option if you plan to machine quilt is pin basting. Pin the quilt layers together with safety pins placed about 3″ or 4″ apart. Begin basting in the center, and move toward the edges first in vertical, then horizontal, rows. Try not to pin directly on the intended quilting lines.

If you plan to hand quilt, baste the layers together with thread using a long needle and light-colored thread. Knot one end of the thread. Using stitches approximately the length of the needle, begin in the center and move out toward the edges in vertical and horizontal rows approximately 4″ apart. Add two diagonal rows of basting.

quilting

Quilting, whether by machine or hand, enhances the pieced or appliquéd design of the quilt. You may choose to quilt in-the-ditch, echo the pieced or appliquéd motifs, use patterns from quilting design books and stencils, or do your own free-motion quilting. Remember to check your batting manufacturer's recommendations for how close the quilting lines must be.

Should you choose to have your quilt professionally longarm quilted, consult with the quilter about their specific requirements, such as the quilt top and backing preparations and the batting and thread choices.

binding

Trim excess batting and backing from the quilt even with the edges of the quilt top, squaring up if necessary.

Making Double-Fold Crosswise Binding

Cut the binding strips crosswise (WOF), and piece them together with diagonal seams to make a continuous binding strip. Trim the seam allowances to ¼″. Press the seams open. Press the entire strip in half lengthwise with wrong sides together.

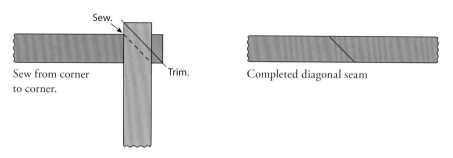

Sew.

Sew from corner to corner.

Trim.

Completed diagonal seam

Attaching the Binding

With the raw edges even, pin the binding to the front edge of the quilt a few inches away from a corner, and leave the first 8″–10″ of the binding un-attached. Start sewing using a ¼″ seam allowance.

Stop ¼″ away from the first corner (see Step 1). Lift your presser foot, pivot 45°, and continue stitching toward the corner and off the quilt. Rotate the quilt one-quarter turn. Fold the binding at a right angle so it extends straight above the quilt and the fold forms a 45° angle in the corner (see Step 2). Then bring the binding strip down even with the edge of the quilt (see Step 3). Begin sewing at the folded edge. Repeat in the same manner at all corners.

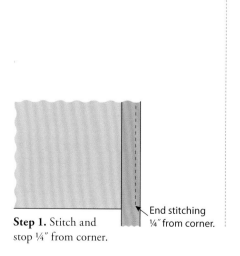

Step 1. Stitch and stop ¼″ from corner.

End stitching ¼″ from corner.

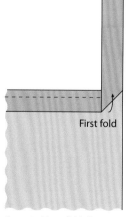

First fold

Step 2. First fold for miter

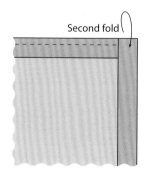

Second fold

Step 3. Second fold alignment

Continue stitching until 10″–12″ from where the binding was first sewn down to the quilt. Overlap the binding tails, and at a point near the middle of the starting and stopping points, cut the binding tails so that they lap over 2½″ (the width of the cut binding strip).

Open both tails. Place one tail on top of the other tail at right angles, right sides together. Mark a diagonal line from corner to corner, and stitch on the line. Check that the binding fits the quilt; then trim the seam allowance to ¼″. Press open.

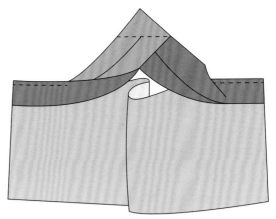

Stitch ends of binding diagonally.

Refold the binding, and stitch this binding section in place on the quilt. Fold the binding over the raw edges to the quilt back. Hand stitch in place, mitering the corners.

+++

labeling

Be sure to add a label on the back of the quilt before giving it to a loved one.

patterns

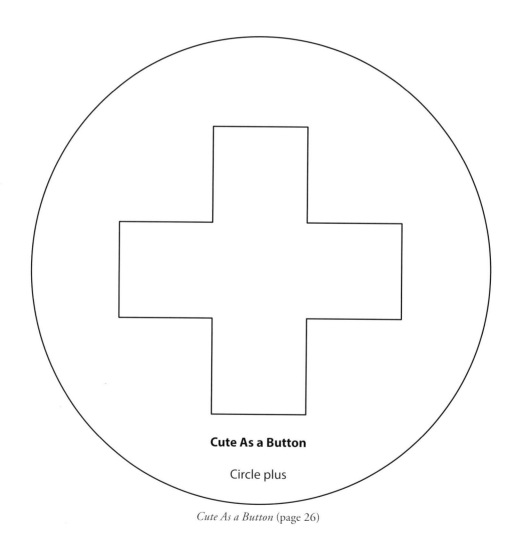

Cute As a Button

Circle plus

Cute As a Button (page 26)

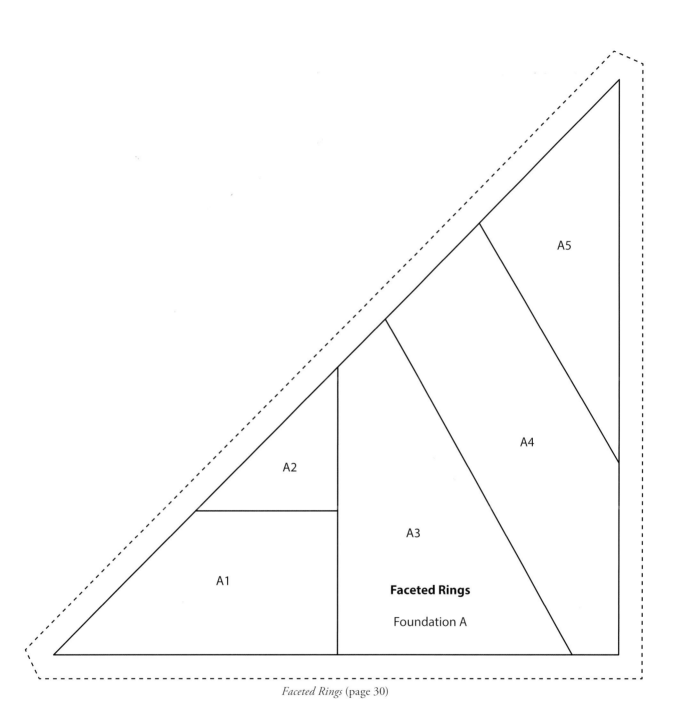

A5

A2

A4

A3

A1

Faceted Rings

Foundation A

Faceted Rings (page 30)

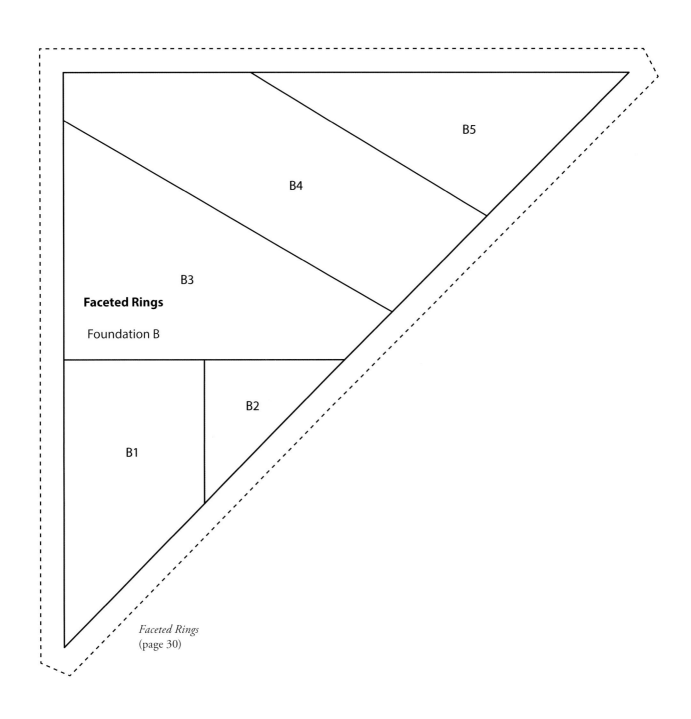

B5

B4

B3

Faceted Rings

Foundation B

B2

B1

Faceted Rings
(page 30)

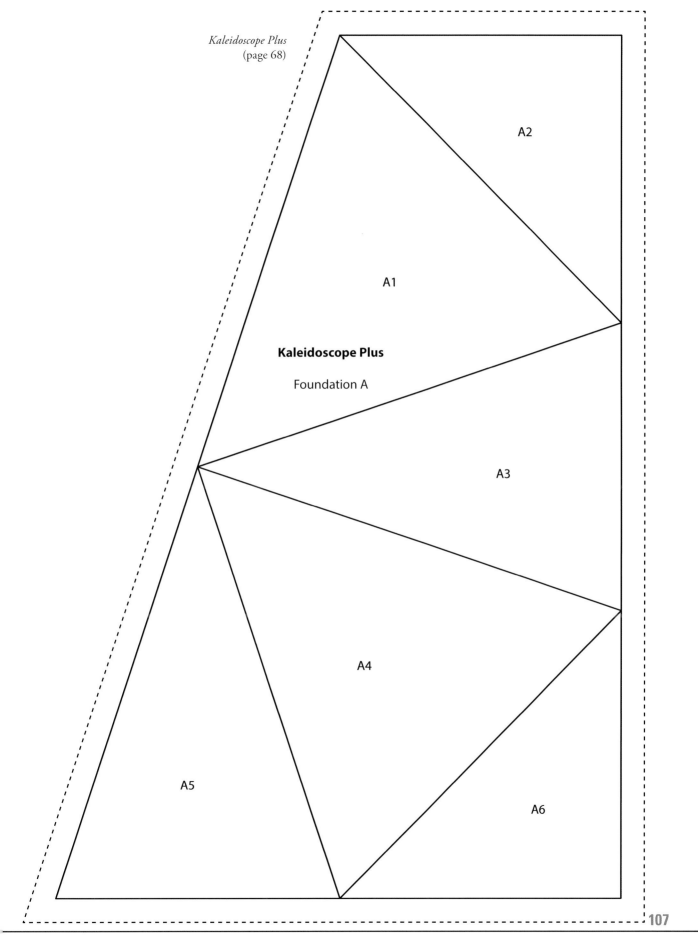

Kaleidoscope Plus
(page 68)

Kaleidoscope Plus

Foundation A

A1

A2

A3

A4

A5

A6

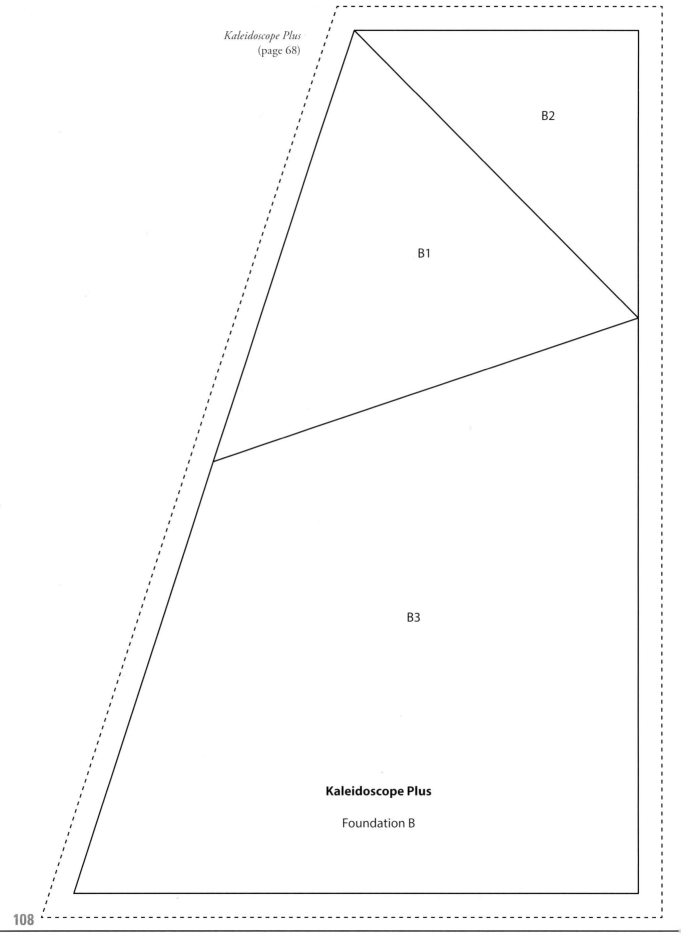

Kaleidoscope Plus
(page 68)

B2

B1

B3

Kaleidoscope Plus

Foundation B

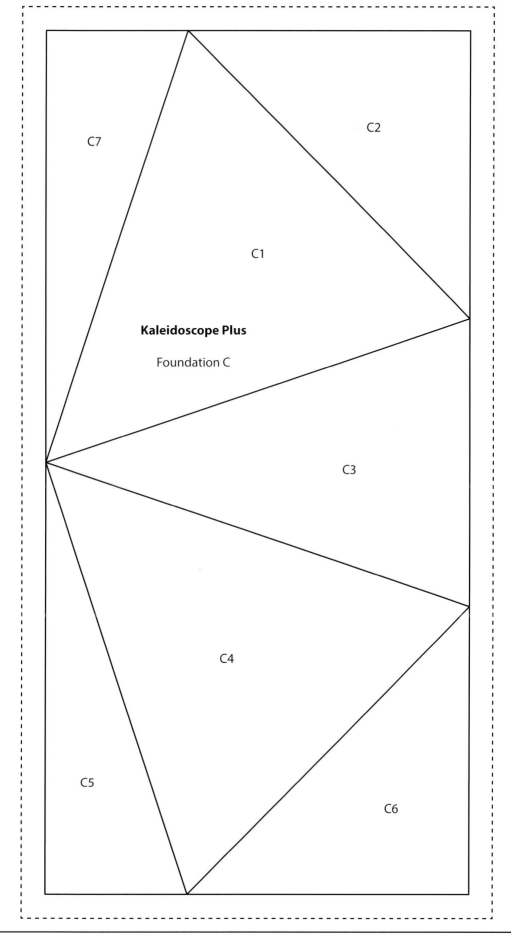

Kaleidoscope Plus

Foundation C

C7

C2

C1

C3

C4

C5

C6

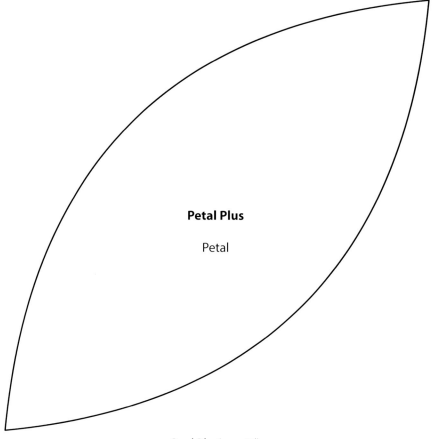

Petal Plus

Petal

Petal Plus (page 84)

about the authors

Cheryl Brickey started quilting in 2010 to make her daughter (then a toddler) a quilt for her first bed, and she has been quilting nonstop  since. Cheryl was born and raised in New Jersey and now calls South Carolina home, where she and her husband are raising their two children. She has a chemical engineering degree and spends her days writing patent applications for a private textile and chemical company. Cheryl uses her technical writing and math skills in each of her designs, with quilt math being one of her favorite elements to pattern writing.

Cheryl is an active member of her local traditional and modern guilds and is very involved with the online quilting community. She has won numerous awards for her quilts and designs. Cheryl has also been featured on the *Moda Bake Shop* blog; in *Modern Quilts Unlimited*, *Quiltmaker*, *Make Modern*, *Quilty*, and *Fat Quarterly* magazines; and in QuiltCon and other international quilt shows.

Follow Cheryl on social media:

Website: meadowmistdesigns.blogspot.com

Instagram: @meadowmistdesigns

Paige Alexander acquired the beginning skills for sewing at a young age while sitting on her grandmother's knee at her 1949 Singer.  While Paige was crafty growing up in northwest Mississippi (and even made a Trip Around the World baby quilt—without a pattern—for a cousin while in college), she truly began her quilting journey in 2003 after window shopping at a quilt shop in upstate South Carolina. Paige quickly joined her local quilt guild, UpCountry Quilters Guild in Pickens, where she has served in many roles including president and treasurer and was instrumental in the formation of the local Greenville chapter of the Modern Quilt Guild.

Paige's attention to detail, precision, and design work has earned her awards from international quilt shows including the American Quilter's Society, National Quilting Association, and the Modern Quilt Guild's QuiltCon. Paige lives with her husband in Easley, South Carolina, on his family's century-old farm surrounded by pine trees.

Follow Paige on social media:

Website: quiltedblooms.com

Instagram: @quiltedblooms

Want even more creative content?

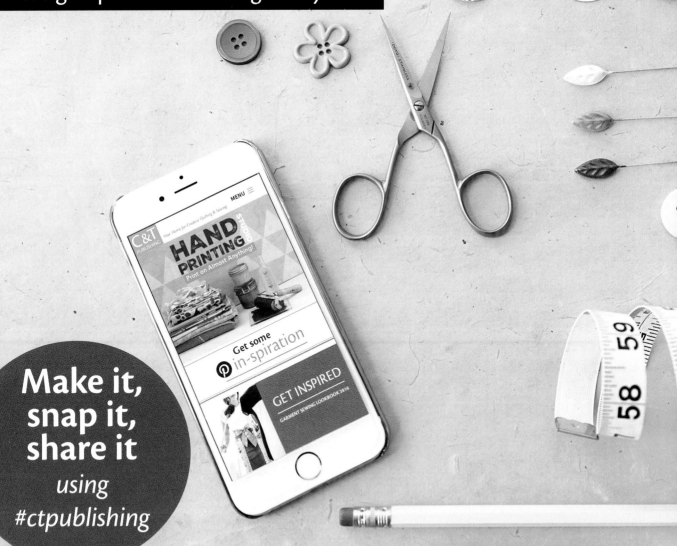